SCRIPTURE
ALONE

Also in the R. C. Sproul Library

The Hunger for Significance

The King without a Shadow

The Glory of Christ

The Soul's Quest for God

The Intimate Marriage

The Invisible Hand

Choosing My Religion

Ultimate Issues

SCRIPTURE
ALONE

The Evangelical Doctrine

R. C. SPROUL

Introduction by Keith A. Mathison

P U B L I S H I N G
P.O. BOX 817 • PHILLIPSBURG • NEW JERSEY 08865-0817

Scripture quotations from the HOLY BIBLE, NEW KING JAMES VERSION (so identified in the index of Scripture) are copyright © 1979, 1980, 1982, by Thomas Nelson, Inc. Scripture quotations in *The Chicago Statement on Biblical Inerrancy* are from the HOLY BIBLE, NEW INTERNATIONAL VERSION®. NIV®. Copyright © 1973, 1978, 1984 by International Bible Society. Used by permission of Zondervan Publishing House. All rights reserved.

Chapter 1 originally appeared in *The Foundation of Biblical Authority*, ed. James Montgomery Boice (Grand Rapids: Zondervan, 1978), pp. 103–119. Reprinted by permission of Linda Boice.

Chapter 2 originally appeared in *Sola Scriptura! The Protestant Position on the Bible*, ed. Don Kistler (Morgan, Pa.: Soli Deo Gloria, 1995), pp. 63–95. Reprinted by permission.

Chapter 3 originally appeared in *God's Inerrant Word: An International Symposium on the Trustworthiness of Scripture*, ed. John Warwick Montgomery (Minneapolis: Bethany, 1974), pp. 242–61. Reprinted by permission of Bethany, Baker Publishing Group.

Chapter 4 originally appeared in *Inerrancy*, ed. Norman L. Geisler (Grand Rapids: Zondervan, 1980), pp. 337–54. Reprinted by permission of the Zondervan Corporation. Scripture quotations changed from NIV to NKJV.

Part 2 appeared most recently as *Explaining Inerrancy* (Orlando: Ligonier Ministries, 1996). Reprinted by permission of Ligonier Ministries.

Appendix 1, *The Ligonier Statement*, was formulated at the Conference on the Inspiration and Authority of Scripture, October 26, 1973, in Ligonier, Pennsylvania.

Appendix 2, *The Chicago Statement on Biblical Inerrancy*, was copyrighted in 1978 by the International Council on Biblical Inerrancy.

Page design and typesetting by Lakeside Design Plus

Printed in the United States of America

Library of Congress Cataloging-in-Publication Data
Sproul, R. C. (Robert Charles), 1939–
    Scripture alone : the evangelical doctrine / R.C. Sproul ; introduction by Keith A. Mathison.
        p.   cm. – (R. C. Sproul library)
    Includes bibliographical references (p.) and indexes.
    Contents: Sola Scriptura – The establishment of Scripture – The case for inerrancy – The internal testimony of the Holy Spirit – The Word of God and authority – The Word of God and revelation – The Word of God and inspiration – The Word of God and inerrancy – The Word of God and truth – The Word of God and you.
    ISBN-10 1-59638-010-1
    ISBN-13 978-1-59638-010-3
    1. Bible—Evidences, authority, etc. 2. Bible—Inspiration 3. Reformed Church—Doctrines.   I. Title.

BS480.S66 2005
220.1'3—dc22

2005047400

CONTENTS

Appendixes

INTRODUCTION

Keith A. Mathison

---

n every generation, certain doctrines have come under attack by those outside as well as by those inside the church. And in every generation certain men have been called to defend the truth. In the twentieth century, the orthodox doctrine of Scripture became a particular focus of intense criticism. The seeds of this modern attack were sown during the Enlightenment with the rise of an autonomous view of human reason. Although these seeds began to bear their bitter fruit in the church almost immediately, they did not begin to come to full fruition until the rise of theological liberalism in the nineteenth century. The reverberations of this liberalism are still being felt today.

In the late nineteenth and early twentieth centuries, scholars teaching at Princeton Theological Seminary produced some of the most important work in defense of the orthodox doctrine of Scripture. One of the most important of these scholars was Benjamin Breckinridge Warfield, whose book *The Inspiration and Authority of the Bible* remains a classic to this day.[1] The conservative orthodox tradition of Princeton Seminary, unfortunately, would not survive the theological battles of the early twentieth century. As a result of the fundamentalist-modernist controversy and the reorganization of Princeton Seminary, many of its conservative faculty, under the leadership of J. Gresham Machen, formed Westminster Theological Seminary in 1929 to carry on the original theological vision of old Princeton. In 1946 the faculty of Westminster Seminary produced a symposium entitled *The Infallible Word*.[2] In 1957 one of the contributors to that volume, Old Testament professor Edward J. Young, wrote a substantial defense of biblical infallibility and inerrancy entitled *Thy Word Is Truth*.[3]

Throughout the middle of the twentieth century, the effects of neoorthodoxy began to become more and more evident within American Christianity. Disciples of Karl Barth and Emil Brunner educated an entire generation of scholars. The result was a predictable move among many professing evangelicals away from the traditional doctrines of biblical infallibility and inerrancy. One of the most dramatic moves occurred in the early 1960s when Fuller Theological Seminary, a professedly evangelical school, abandoned its commitment to the doctrine of inerrancy.[4]

Many people recognized the slide away from orthodoxy that was occurring within Evangelicalism itself and were rightly concerned.[5] Not all of them, however, were called to take a leadership role in turning the tide. One of those who was called to such a role was a young theologian in Pennsylvania named R. C. Sproul. Dr. Sproul had opened the

LigonierValley Study Center in 1971 for the purpose of providing biblical and theological training that went beyond the level possible in a Sunday school setting. In 1973 he invited a number of prominent evangelical scholars to meet in Ligonier, Pennsylvania, to present a series of papers on the subject of biblical inerrancy. In the fall of 1973, the Ligonier Conference on the Inspiration and Authority of Scripture convened. In 1974 the papers that were presented at the conference were edited by John Warwick Montgomery and published in the book *God's Inerrant Word.*[6] The conference also produced The Ligonier Statement, a brief statement of faith on the subject of biblical authority.

Dr. Sproul's leadership role did not end with the Ligonier Conference. At an apologetics conference in California, he mentioned the Ligonier Conference to the other men present and explained that he thought it would be a good idea to go national with a council on inerrancy. As a result of these early discussions, the International Council on Biblical Inerrancy (ICBI) was formed in 1977. The council was formed to defend the doctrine of inerrancy and to counter the drift away from this doctrine in churches and seminaries. The members of the council produced a number of books on various issues related to the doctrine of inerrancy. In 1978 the council produced what is perhaps its most important work, The Chicago Statement on Biblical Inerrancy. Dr. Sproul was on the committee that produced this important statement, and he was chosen as well to write a brief commentary on each article of the statement. Ligonier Ministries later published this commentary under the title *Explaining Inerrancy.*[7]

The ICBI brought the issue of inerrancy to the forefront of evangelical discussion and debate. As a result of the council's work, some seminaries strengthened their commitment to biblical inerrancy. Other seminaries continued to slide. Although the council ended its formal work in 1987, the work of defending the doctrine of inerrancy continues. Dr. Sproul continues to this day to defend the infallible authority of Scripture in his writings, lectures, and sermons. The contents of the present volume contain some of his most significant writings on the doctrine of Scripture.

The four chapters in part 1 are reprints of Dr. Sproul's contributions to several important books on the subject of biblical authority. The first chapter, "*Sola Scriptura:* Crucial to Evangelicalism," examines the formal cause of the Reformation—the doctrine of *sola Scriptura*—and explores the relationship between this doctrine and the doctrine of inerrancy. Dr. Sproul explains that the doctrine of inerrancy is of crucial importance to the Christian faith and examines some of the many problems that arise from a doctrine of limited inerrancy.

The second chapter, "The Establishment of Scripture," focuses on the complicated issue of biblical canonicity. Dr. Sproul explains the historical process by which the canon was formed under the providential guidance of God. He also examines some of the faulty views of the canon that are in existence, including various forms of canon reduction and canon addition.

Chapter 3, "The Case for Inerrancy: A Methodological Analysis," provides a methodological framework for a defense of biblical inerrancy. Dr. Sproul first examines and critiques the "confessional" method of G. C. Berkouwer and the "presuppositional" method of Cornelius Van Til before proceeding to an in-depth examination of the "classical" method for defending biblical inerrancy.

The final chapter in part 1, "The Internal Testimony of the Holy Spirit," explains how the internal testimony of the Holy Spirit confirms the reliability of Scripture and gives us certainty that it is God's Word. Dr. Sproul examines in particular the work of John Calvin on the subject and provides a thorough critique of the neoorthodox view taught by men such as Emil Brunner.

Part 2 contains Dr. Sproul's detailed commentary on the nineteen articles of the Chicago Statement on Biblical Inerrancy that was adopted by the ICBI in 1978. This commentary provides a fuller explanation and exposition of each of the articles in order to clarify the precise position of the council.

The trustworthiness of God's Word has been attacked since the serpent asked the question, "Hath God said?" It continues to be attacked in various and subtle ways in our own day. It will continue to be attacked until Christ has put all enemies under his feet on the last day. The Christian church, then, must continue to resist all such attacks. This collection of Dr. Sproul's writings on the doctrine of biblical authority is provided in the hope that it may assist a new generation of Christians to stand firm in defense of the truth.

PART 1

TOWARD A DOCTRINE
of
SCRIPTURE

1

SOLA SCRIPTURA:
CRUCIAL TO EVANGELICALISM

he only source and norm of all Christian knowledge is the Holy Scripture.[1] This thematic statement introduces *De Scriptura Sacra* of Heinrich
Heppe's classic work in Reformed dogmatics and provides
a succinct expression of the Reformation slogan *sola Scriptura.* The two key words that are used to crystalize the *sola*
character of Scripture are *source* and *norm.*

The Reformation principle of *sola Scriptura* was given the
status of the formal cause of the Reformation by Phillip
Melanchthon and his Lutheran followers. The formal cause
was distinguished from the material cause of *sola fide* (by
faith alone). Though the chief theological issue of the Reformation was the question of the matter of justification, the
controversy touched heavily on the underlying question of
authority. As is usually the case in theological controversy,
the issue of ultimate authority lurked in the background
(though it was by no means hidden or obscure) of Martin

Luther's struggle with Rome over justification. The question of the *source* of Luther's doctrine and the normative authority by which it was to be judged was vital to his cause.

Sola Scriptura and Inerrancy

A brief historical recapitulation of the steps that led to Luther's *sola Scriptura* dictum may be helpful. After Luther posted his Ninety-Five Theses in 1517, a series of debates, correspondence, charges, and countercharges ensued, culminating in Luther's dramatic stand at Worms in April 1521. The two most significant transitional points between the theses of 1517 and the Diet of Worms of 1521 were the debates at Augsburg and Leipzig.

In October 1518 Luther met with Cardinal Cajetan of the Dominicans. Cajetan was acknowledged to be the most learned theologian of the Roman Curia. In the course of their discussions Cajetan was able to elicit from Luther his views on the infallibility of the pope. Luther asserted that the pope could err and claimed that Pope Clement VI's bull *Unigenitus* (1343) was contrary to Scripture.[2]

In the summer of 1519 the dramatic encounter between Luther and Johannes von Eck took place at Leipzig. In this exchange Eck elicited from Luther the admission of his belief that not only could the pope err but church councils could and did err as well. It was at Leipzig that Luther made clear his assertion: Scripture alone is the ultimate, divine authority in all matters pertaining to religion. Gordon Rupp gives the following account:

16

Luther affirmed that "among the articles of John Huss and the Hussites which were condemned, are many which are truly Christian and evangelical, and which the church universal cannot condemn!" This was sensational! There was a moment of shocked silence, and then an uproar above which could be heard Duke George's disgusted, "Gad, Sir, that's the Plague! . . ." Eck pressed his advantage home, and Luther, trapped, admitted that since their decrees are also of human law, Councils may err.[3]

So by the time Luther stood before the Diet of Worms, the principle of *sola Scriptura* was already well established in his mind and work. Only the Scripture carries absolute normative authority. Why? For Luther the *sola* of *sola Scriptura* was inseparably related to the Scriptures' unique inerrancy. It was because popes could and did err and because councils could and did err that Luther came to realize the supremacy of Scripture. Luther did not despise church authority nor did he repudiate church councils as having no value. His praise of the Council of Nicea is noteworthy. Luther and the Reformers did not mean by *sola Scriptura* that the Bible is the only authority in the church. Rather, they meant that the Bible is the only *infallible* authority in the church. Paul Althaus summarizes the train of Luther's thought by saying:

> We may trust unconditionally only in the Word of God and not in the teaching of the fathers; for the teachers of the Church can err and have erred. Scripture never errs. Therefore it alone has unconditional authority. The authority of the theologians of the Church is relative and conditional.

17

> Without the authority of the words of Scripture, no one can establish hard and fast statements in the Church.[4]

Thus Althaus sees Luther's principle of *sola Scriptura* arising as a corollary of the inerrancy of Scripture. To be sure, the fact that Scripture is elevated to be the sole authority of the church does not carry with it the necessary inference that it is inerrant. It could be asserted that councils, popes, and the Bible all err[5] and still postulate a theory of *sola Scriptura*. Scripture could be considered on a *primus inter pares* ("first among equals") basis with ecclesiastical authority, giving it a kind of primacy among errant sources. Or Scripture could be regarded as carrying unique authority solely on the basis of its being the primary historical source of the gospel. But the Reformers' view of *sola Scriptura* was higher than this. The Reformation principle of *sola Scriptura* involved inerrancy.[6]

Sola Scriptura, ascribing to the Scriptures a unique authority, must be understood in a normative sense. Not descriptive, but rather normative authority is meant by the formula. The normative character of the *sola Scriptura* principle may be seen by a brief survey of sixteenth-century Reformed confessions.[7] The Theses of Berne (1528):

> The Church of Christ makes no laws or commandments without God's Word. Hence all human traditions, which are called ecclesiastical commandments, are binding upon us only in so far as they are based on and commanded by God's Word. (Sec. 2)

The Geneva Confession (1536):

First we affirm that we desire to follow Scripture alone as a rule of faith and religion, without mixing with it any other things which might be devised by the opinion of men apart from the Word of God, and without wishing to accept for our spiritual government any other doctrine than what is conveyed to us by the same Word without addition or diminution, according to the command of our Lord (Sec. 1).

The French Confession of Faith (1559):

We believe that the Word contained in these books has proceeded from God, and receives its authority from him alone, and not from men. And inasmuch as it is the rule of all truth, containing all that is necessary for the service of God and for our salvation, it is not lawful for men, nor even for angels, to add to it, to take away from it, or to change it. Whence it follows that no authority, whether of antiquity, or custom, or numbers, or human wisdom, or judgments, or proclamations, or edicts, or decrees, or councils, or visions, or miracles, should be opposed to these Holy Scriptures, but on the contrary, all things should be examined, regulated, and reformed according to them. (Art. 5)

The Belgic Confession (1561):

We receive all these books, and these only, as holy and confirmation of our faith; believing, without any doubt, all things contained in them, not so much because the church receives and approves them as such, but more especially because the Holy Ghost witnessed in our hearts that they are from God, whereof they carry the evidence in themselves (Art. 5).

> Therefore we reject with all our hearts whatsoever doth not agree with this infallible rule (Art. 7).

The Second Helvetic Confession (1566):

> Therefore, we do not admit any other judge than Christ himself, who proclaims by the Holy Scriptures what is true, what is false, what is to be followed, or what is to be avoided (Chap. 2).

Uniformly the sixteenth-century confessions elevate the authority of Scripture over any other conceivable authority. Thus, even the testimony of angels is to be judged by the Scriptures. Why? Because, as Luther believed, the Scriptures alone are inerrant. *Sola Scriptura* as the supreme norm of ecclesiastical authority rests ultimately on the premise of the infallibility of the Word of God.

Extent of the Norm

To what extent does the *sola Scriptura* principle of authority apply? We hear statements that declare Scripture to be the "only infallible rule of faith and practice." Does this limit the scope of biblical infallibility? Among advocates of limited inerrancy we hear the popular notion that the Bible is inerrant or infallible only when it speaks of matters of faith and practice. Matters of history or cosmology may contain error, but not matters of faith and practice. Here we see a subtle shift from the Reformation principle. Note the difference in the following propositions:

20

A. The Bible is the only infallible rule of faith and practice.

B. The Bible is infallible only when it speaks of faith and practice.

In premise A, "faith and practice" are generic terms that describe the Bible. In premise B, "faith and practice" presumably describe only a particular part of the Bible. Premise A affirms that there is but one infallible authority for the church. The proposition sets no content limit on the infallibility of the Scriptures. Premise B gives a reduced canon of that which is infallible; that is, the Bible is infallible only when it speaks of faith and practice. This second premise represents a clear and decisive departure from the Reformation view.

Premise A does not say that the Bible provides information about every area of life, such as mathematics or physics. But it affirms that what the Bible teaches, it teaches infallibly.

The Source of Authority

Heinrich Heppe's *sola* indicates that the Bible is not only the unique and final authority of the church but is also the "only source of all Christian knowledge." At first glance this statement may seem to suggest that the only source of revelation open to man is that found in Scripture. But that is not the intent of Heppe's statement, nor is it the intent of the Reformation principle of *sola Scriptura*.

Uniformly the Reformers acknowledged general revelation as a source of knowledge of God. The question of whether or not that general revelation yields a bona fide natural theology was and is widely disputed, but there is no serious doubt that the Reformers affirmed a revelation present in nature.[8] Thus the *sola* does not exclude general revelation but points beyond it to the sufficiency of Scripture as the unique source of written special revelation.

The context of the *sola Scriptura* schema with respect to source was the issue (raised over against Rome) regarding the relationship of Scripture and tradition. Central to the debate was the Council of Trent's declaration regarding Scripture and tradition. (Trent was part of the Roman counteroffensive to the Reformation, and the *sola Scriptura* was not passed over lightly in this counteroffensive.) In the fourth session of the Council of Trent the following decree was formulated:

> This (Gospel), of old promised through the Prophets in the Holy Scriptures, our Lord Jesus Christ, the Son of God, promulgated first with His own mouth, and then commanded it to be preached by His Apostles to every creature as the source at once of all saving truth and rules of conduct. It also clearly perceives that these truths and rules are contained *in the written books and in the unwritten traditions*, which, received by the Apostles from the mouth of Christ Himself, or from the Apostles themselves, the Holy Ghost dictating, have come down to us, transmitted as it were from hand to hand. Following then, the examples of the Orthodox fathers, it receives and venerates with a feeling of piety and reverence all the books both of the Old and New Testaments, since one God is the author of both; also the traditions, whether they relate to faith or to morals, as having been dictated either orally by Christ or by the Holy Ghost, and preserved in the Catholic church in unbroken succession.[9]

22

In this decree the Roman Catholic church apparently affirmed *two* sources of special revelation—Scripture and the tradition of the church—although in recent years this "dual source" theory has come into question within the Roman church.

G. C. Berkouwer's work on Vatican Council II provides a lengthy discussion of current interpretations of the Tridentine formula on Scripture and tradition. Some scholars argue that tradition adds no new content to Scripture but merely serves either as a depository in the life of the church or as a formal interpretive tool of the church.[10] A technical point of historical research concerning Trent sheds some interesting light on the matter. In the original draft of the fourth session of Trent the decree read that "the truths . . . are contained partly [*partim*] in Scripture and partly [*partim*] in the unwritten traditions." But at a decisive point in the council's deliberations two priests, Nacchianti and Bonnucio, rose in protest against the *partim . . . partim* formula. These men protested on the grounds that this view would destroy the uniqueness and sufficiency of Scripture.[11] All we know from that point on is that the words *partly . . . partly* were removed from the text and replaced by the word *and* (*et*). Did this mean that the council responded to the protest and perhaps left the relationship between Scripture and tradition purposely ambiguous? Was the change stylistic, meaning that the council still maintained two distinct sources of revelation? These questions are the focus of the current debate among Roman theologians.

One thing is certain. The Roman church has interpreted Trent as affirming two sources of special revelation since the sixteenth century. Vatican I spoke of two sources. The papal encyclical *Humani Generis* spoke of "sources of revelation."[12] Even Pope John XXIII spoke of Scripture *and* tradition in *Ad Petri Cathedram*.[13]

Not only has the dual-source theory been confirmed both by ecumenical councils and papal encyclicals, but tradition has been appealed to on countless occasions to validate doctrinal formulations that divide Rome and Protestantism. This is particularly true regarding decisions in the area of Mariology.

Over against this dual-source theory stands the *sola* of *sola Scriptura*. Again, the Reformers did not despise the treasury of church tradition. The great councils of Nicea, Ephesus, Chalcedon, and Constantinople receive much honor in Protestant tradition. The Reformers themselves gave tribute to the insights of the church fathers. John Calvin's love for Augustine is apparent throughout the *Institutes of the Christian Religion*. Luther's expertise in the area of Patristics was evident in his debates with Cajetan and Eck. He frequently quotes the fathers as highly respected ecclesiastical authorities. But the difference is this: For the Reformers no church council, synod, classical theologian, or early church father is regarded as infallible. All are open to correction and critique. We have no *Doctor Irrefragabilis* of Protestantism.

Protestant churches have tended to be confessional in character. Subscription to confessions and creeds has been mandatory for the clergy and parish of many denominations. Confessions have been used as a test of orthodoxy and conformity to the faith and practice of the church. But the confessions are all regarded as reformable. They are considered reformable because they are considered fallible. But the *sola Scriptura* principle in its classic application regards the Scripture as irreformable because of its infallibility.

Thus the two primary thrusts of *sola Scriptura* point to (1) Scripture's uniqueness as normative authority and (2) its uniqueness as the source of special revelation. Norm and source are the twin implicates of the *sola Scriptura* principle.

Is *Sola Scriptura* the Essence of Christianity?

In a recent publication on questions of Scripture, Bernard Ramm wrote an essay entitled "Is 'Scripture Alone' the Essence of Christianity?" Using the nineteenth-century German penchant for the quest of the *wesen* of Christianity as a jumping-off point, Ramm gives a brief history of the liberal-conservative controversy concerning the role of Scripture in the Christian faith. Defining *wesen* as "the essence of something, the real spirit or burden of a treatise, the heart of the matter," he concludes that Scripture is not the *wesen* of Christianity. He provides a historical survey to indicate that neither the Reformers nor the strong advocates of inerrancy, A. A. Hodge and B. B. Warfield, believed that *sola Scriptura* was the essence of Christianity. Ramm cites numerous quotations from Hodge and Warfield that speak of the Scriptures as being "absolutely infallible" and "without error of facts or doctrines." Yet these men affirmed that "Christianity was true independently of any theory of inspiration, and its great doctrines were believable within themselves."[14]

Ramm goes on to express grave concern about the present debate among evangelicals concerning inerrancy. Here his concern focuses not on the teaching of Hodge and Warfield but on the attitudes of their contemporary disciples who, in Ramm's opinion, go beyond their forefathers in asserting a particular view of Scripture as being Christianity's essence. Ramm writes:

> From the other writings of Warfield in particular, it would be impossible to say that he identified the *Wesen* of Christianity with his view of Holy Scripture. He was enough of a historian of theology to avoid saying that. The "inspiration" article was an essay in strategy. However, among current followers of the so-called Warfield position there have been certain shifts away from the original strategic stance of the essay. One's doctrine of Scripture has become now the first and most important doctrine, one's theory of the *Wesen* of Christianity, so that all other doctrines have validity now only as they are part of the inerrant Scripture. Thus evangelical teachers, or evangelical schools or evangelical movements, can be judged as to whether or not they are true to the *Wesen* of Christianity by their theory of inspiration. It can be stated even more directly: an evangelical has made a theory of inspiration the *Wesen* of Christianity if he assumes that the most important doctrine in a man's theology, and most revelatory of the entire range of his theological thought, is his theology of inspiration.[15]

It appears from this statement that the "essence" of Ramm's concern for the present state of evangelicalism is that one's doctrine of Scripture is viewed as the essence or *wesen* of Christianity. This writer can only join hands with Ramm in total agreement with his concern. To make one's view of Scripture in general or of inspiration in particular the essence of Christianity would be to commit an error of the most severe magnitude. To subordinate the importance of the gospel itself to the importance of our historical source book of it would be to obscure the centrality of Christ. To subordinate *sola fide* to *sola Scriptura* would be to misunderstand radically the *wesen* of the Reformation. Clearly Ramm is correct in taking his stand on this point with Hodge, Warfield, and the Reformers. Who can object to that?

One may be troubled, however, by a portion of Ramm's stated concern. Who are these "current followers" of Warfield who in fact do maintain that *sola Scriptura* is the heart or essence of Christianity? What disciple of Warfield's has ever maintained that *sola Scriptura* is essential to salvation? Ramm provides us with no names or documentary evidence to demonstrate that his deep concern is warranted.

To be sure, strong statements have been made by followers of the Warfield school of the crucial importance of *sola Scriptura* and the centrality of biblical authority to all theological disputes. Perhaps these statements have contained some "overkill" in the passion of debate, which is always regrettable. We must be very cautious in our zeal to defend a high view of Scripture not to give the impression that we are talking about an article on which our salvation depends.[16]

We can cite the following statements by advocates of the Warfield school that could be construed as a possible basis for Ramm's concern. In *God's Inerrant Word*, J. I. Packer makes the following assertion: "What Luther thus voiced at Worms shows the essential motivation and concern, theological and religious, of the entire Reformation movement: namely that the Word of God alone must rule, and no Christian man dare do other than allow it to enthrone itself in his conscience and heart."[17] Here Packer calls the notion of *sola*

27

Scriptura "the essential motivation and concern" of the Reformation. In itself this quote certainly suggests that Packer views *sola Scriptura* as *the* essence of the Reformation.

However, in defense of Packer it must be noted that to say *sola Scriptura* was the essential motivation of the Reformation movement is not to say that *sola Scriptura* is the essence of Christianity. He is speaking here of a historical controversy. That *sola Scriptura* was at the heart of the controversy and central to the debate cannot be doubted. To say that *sola Scriptura* was *an* essential motif or concern of the Reformation cannot be doubted. That it was *the essential* concern may be brought into question; this may be regarded as an overstatement. But again, in fairness to Packer, it must be noted that earlier in his essay he had already indicated that *justification by faith alone* was the material principle. So he had already maintained that *sola Scriptura* was subordinate to *sola fide* in the controversy.[18] In any case, though the word *essential* is used, there is no hint here that Packer maintains that *sola Scriptura* is *the* essence of Christianity.

In a recent unpublished essay, Richard Lovelace of Gordon-Conwell Theological Seminary cites both Harold Lindsell and Francis Schaeffer as men who have sounded urgent warnings concerning the relationship between inerrancy and evangelicalism. Lovelace cites the following statements of Schaeffer:

> There is no use of evangelicalism seeming to get larger and larger, if at the same time appreciable parts . . . are getting soft at that which is the central core, namely the Scriptures. . . . We must . . . say most lovingly but clearly: evangelical-

ism is not consistently evangelical unless there is a line drawn between those who take a full view of Scripture and those who do not.[19]

Again Schaeffer is cited: "Holding to a strong view of Scripture or not holding to it is the watershed of the evangelical world."[20] In these statements Francis Schaeffer maintains that the Scriptures are (1) the "central core" of Evangelicalism, (2) a mark of "consistent Evangelicalism," and (3) the "watershed of the evangelical world." These are strong assertions about the role of *sola Scriptura*, but they are made with reference to Evangelicalism, not Christianity (though I am sure Schaeffer believes Evangelicalism is the purest expression of Christianity to be found). Evangelicalism refers to a historical position or movement. When he speaks of "watersheds," he is speaking of crucial historical turning points. When he speaks of "consistent" Evangelicalism, he implies there may be such a thing as inconsistent Evangelicalism.

The troublesome quote of Schaeffer is that one in which he says the Scriptures are "the central core" of Evangelicalism. Here "core" is in singular with the definite article giving it a *sola* character. Does Schaeffer mean that the Bible is the core of Evangelicalism and the gospel is the husk? Is *sola Scriptura* the center and *sola fide* at the periphery of Evangelicalism? It is hard to think that Schaeffer would make such an assertion. Indeed, one may question if Schaeffer means what he in fact does say here. Had he said, "Scripture is *at* the core of Evangelicalism," there would be no dispute. But to say it *is* the core appears an overstatement.

29

Perhaps we have here a slip of the pen, which any of us can and frequently do make.

In similar fashion Harold Lindsell may be quoted: "Is the term 'evangelical' broad enough in its meaning to include within it believers in inerrancy and believers in an inerrancy limited to matters of faith and practice?"[21] Lindsell raises the question of whether or not inerrancy of the entire Bible is essential to the term *evangelical*. The question raised is: If *sola Scriptura* in its fullest sense is of the *wesen* of Evangelicalism, can one who espouses limited inerrancy be genuinely called *evangelical*? The issue is the meaning of the term *evangelical*. Does it carry with it the automatic assumption of full inerrancy? Again we must point out the difference between the historical label "evangelical" and what is essential to Christianity.

None of the scholars mentioned have said that adherence to inerrancy or *sola Scriptura* is essential to salvation. None have *sola Scriptura* as the *wesen* of Christianity.

It could be said that the argument of the writer of this chapter is constructed on straw men who "come close" to asserting that *sola Scriptura* is the essence of Christianity but who, in the final analysis, shrink from such an assertion. But it is not my purpose to create straw men. It is simply to find some basis for Ramm's assertion about modern followers of Warfield. Since I have not been able to find any followers of Warfield who assert *sola Scriptura* as the *wesen* of Christianity, the best I can do is to cite examples of statements that could possibly be misconstrued to assert that. It is probably charity that restrained Ramm from naming those he had in mind. But unfortunately, the absence of names casts a shadow of suspicion over all modern followers of Warf who hold to full inerrancy.

Though advocates of inerrancy in the full sense of *sola Scriptura* do not regard it as being essential to salvation, they do maintain that the principle is *crucial* to Christianity and to consistent Evangelicalism. That in Scripture we have divine revelation is no small matter. That the gospel rests not on human conjecture or rational speculation is of vital importance. But there is no quarrel with Ramm on these points. He summarizes his own position by saying:

1. There is no questioning of the sola Scriptura in theology. Scripture is the supreme and final authority in theological decision-making.
2. One's view of revelation, inspiration, and interpretation are important. They do implicate each other. Our discussion rather has been whether a certain view of inspiration could stand as the *Wesen* of Christianity. We have in no manner suggested that matters of revelation, inspiration, and interpretation are unimportant in theology.[22]

Here we delight in agreement with this strong affirmation of the crucial importance of *sola Scriptura*.

Strangely, however, Ramm continues his summary by saying, "If the integrity of other evangelicals, evangelical schools, or evangelical movements is assessed by their view of inspiration, then, for them, inspiration has become the *Wesen* of Christianity."[23] The inference Ramm draws at this point is at once puzzling and astonishing, and perhaps we meet here merely another case of overstatement or a slip of

31

the pen. How would it follow from an assessment of others' Evangelicalism as being consistent or inconsistent according to their view of Scripture that inspiration has become the *wesen* of Christianity? This inference involves a quantum leap of logic.

If the first two points of Ramm's summary are correct— that *sola Scriptura* is important and that it implicates views of interpretation and theological decision making—why should not a school's or movement's integrity (a fully integrated stance) be assessed by this principle? Though *sola Scriptura* is not the *wesen* of Christianity, it is still of crucial importance. If a school or movement softens its view of Scripture, that does not mean it has repudiated the essence of Christianity. But it does mean that a crucial point of doctrine and classical evangelical unity has been compromised. If, as Ramm suggests, one's view of Scripture is so important, then a weakening of that view should concern us.

The issue of full or limited inerrancy is a serious one among those within the framework of historic Evangelicalism. In the past a healthy and energetic spirit of cooperation has existed among evangelicals from various and diverse theological persuasions and ecclesiastical affiliations. Lutherans and Baptists, Calvinists and Arminians, and believers of all sorts have united in evangelical activity. What has been the cohesive force of that unity? In the first instance, there has been a consensus of catholic articles of faith, such as the deity of Christ. In the second instance, a strong point of unity has been the cardinal doctrine of the Protestant Reformation: justification by faith alone. In the last instance, there has been the unifying factor of *sola Scriptura* in the sense of full inerrancy. The only "creed" that has bound the Evangelical Theological Society together, for example, has been the affirmation of inerrancy. Now that point of unity is in jeopardy. The essence of Christianity is not the issue. But a vital point of consistent Evangelicalism is.[24]

Sola Scriptura and Limited Inerrancy

Is *sola Scriptura* compatible with a view of Scripture that limits inerrancy to matters of faith and practice? Theoretically it would seem to be possible if "faith and practice" could be separated from any part of Scripture. So long as biblical teaching regarding faith and practice were held to be normative for the Christian community, there would appear to be no threat to the essence of Christianity. However, certain problems exist with such a view of Scripture that do seriously threaten the essence of Christianity.

The first major problem we encounter with limited inerrancy is the problem of *canon reduction*. The canon or "norm" of Scripture is reduced *de facto* to that content relating to faith and practice. This immediately raises the hermeneutical question concerning what parts of Scripture deal with faith. As evangelicals wrestle among themselves in intramural debates, they must keep one eye focused on the liberal world of biblical scholarship, for the principle of the reduction of canon to matters of "faith" is precisely the chief operative in Rudolf Bultmann's hermeneutic. Bultmann thinks we must clear away the prescientific and faulty historical "husk" of Scripture to get to the viable kernel of "faith." Thus, although Bultmann has no inerrant kernel or *kerygma* to fall back on, his problem of canon reduction remains substantially the same as that of those who limit inerrancy to faith and practice.

Before someone cries foul or cites the informal fallacy of *argumentum ad hominem* (abusive) or the "guilt by association" fallacy, let this concern be clarified. I am not saying that advocates of limited inerrancy are cryptic or even incipient Bultmannians, but that there is one very significant point of similarity between the two schools: *canon reductionism.* Evangelical advocates of limited inerrancy are not expected to embrace Bultmann's mythical view of New Testament supernaturalism. But their method has no inherent safeguard from an arbitrary delimitation of the scope of the biblical canon.

The second serious problem, closely related to the first, is the problem of the relationship of faith and history, perhaps the most serious question of contemporary New Testament scholarship. If we limit the notion of inerrancy to matters of faith and practice, what becomes of biblical history? Is the historical substratum of the gospel negotiable? Are only those portions of the biblical narrative that have a clear bearing on faith inerrant? How do we escape dehistoricizing the gospel and relegating it to a level of supratemporal existential "decision?" We know that the Bible is not an ordinary history book but a book of *redemptive* history. But is it not also a book of redemptive *history?* If we exclude the realm of history from the category of inspiration or inerrancy either in whole or in part, do we not inevitably lose the gospel?

The third problem we face with limiting inerrancy to matters of faith and practice is an apologetic one. To those critics outside the fellowship of evangelicals, the notion of "limited inerrancy" appears artificial and contrived. Limited inerrancy gets us off the apologetical hook by making us immune to religious-historical criticism. We can eat our cake and have it too. The gospel is preserved; and our faith and practice remains intact while we admit errors in matters of history and cosmology. We cannot believe the Bible concerning earthly things, but we stake our lives on what it says concerning heavenly things. That approach was totally abrogated by our Lord (John 3:12).

How do we explain and defend the idea that the Bible is divinely superintended in part of its content but not all of it? Which part is inspired? Why only the faith and practice parts? Again, which are the faith and practice parts? Can we not justly be accused of "weaseling" if we adopt such a view? We remove our faith from the arena of historical verification or falsification. This is a fatal blow for apologetics as the reasoned defense of Christianity.[25]

Finally, we face the problem of the domino theory. Frequently this concern is dismissed out of hand as being so much alarmism. But our doctrine of Scripture is not a child's game of dominoes. We know instances in which men have abandoned belief in full inerrancy but have remained substantially orthodox in the rest of their theology. We are also aware of the sad instances in which full inerrancy is affirmed yet the substance of theology is corrupt. Inerrancy is no guarantee of biblical orthodoxy. Yet even a cursory view of church history has shown some pattern of correlation between a weakening of biblical authority and serious defection regarding the *wesen* of Christianity. The *wesen* of nineteenth-century liberalism is hardly the gospel evangelicals embrace.

We have already seen, within evangelical circles, a move from limited inerrancy to challenges of matters of faith and practice. When the Apostle Paul is depicted as espousing two mutually contradictory views of the role of women in the church, we see a critique of apostolic teaching that does touch directly on the practice of the church.[26] In the hotly disputed issue of homosexuality we see denominational commissions not only supplementing biblical authority with corroborative evidence drawn from modern sources of medical psychological study but also "correcting" the biblical view by such secular authority.[27] The direction of these movements of thought is a matter of grave concern for advocates of full inerrancy.

We face a crisis of authority in the church. It is precisely our faith and our practice that is in question. It is for faith and practice that we defend a fully infallible rule—a total view of *sola Scriptura*.

We know some confusion has existed (much unnecessarily) about the meaning of full inerrancy. But with all the problems of definition that plague the concept, we do not think it has died the death of a thousand qualifications.

We are concerned about *sola Scriptura* for many reasons. But we affirm it in the final analysis not because it was the view of the Reformers, not because we slavishly revere Hodge and Warfield, not even because we are afraid of dominoes or a difficult apologetic. We defend it and express our deep concern about it because we believe it is the truth. It is a truth we do not want to negotiate. We earnestly desire dialogue with our evangelical brothers and colaborers who differ from us. We want to heal the wounds that controversy so frequently brings. We know our own views are by no means inerrant. But we believe inerrancy is true and is of vital importance to our common cause of the gospel.

Further dialogue within the evangelical world should at least help us clarify what real differences there are among us. Such clarification is important if there is to be any hope of resolving those differences. We do not intend to communicate that a person's Christian faith stands or falls with his view of Scripture. We do not question the Christian commitment of advocates of limited inerrancy. What we do question is the correctness of their doctrine of Scripture, as they question ours. But we consider this debate, as serious as it is, a debate between members of the household of God. May our Father bring us to unity here as he has in many glorious affirmations of his gospel.

2

THE ESTABLISHMENT
OF SCRIPTURE

orm of norms and without norm." With these words the historic church confessed her faith in the authority of sacred Scripture. The phrase "norm of norms" was designed to indicate the superlative degree in a manner similar to that expression used in the New Testament for Christ, that he is King of kings and "Lord of lords." To be King of kings is to be supreme King who rules over all lesser kings. To be Lord of lords is to be exalted above all other lords. Likewise the phrase "norm of norms" indicates a norm that is over lesser norms. The additional phrase, "without norm," indicates that the normative character of Scripture is a norm *sui generis*. This norm is in a class by itself. It does not function as a *primus inter pares*, a first among equals.

When we speak of the canon of Scripture we are speaking of a norm or rule. The term *canon* is derived by transliteration from the Greek word *kanon*, which means "a measuring rod," "rule," or "norm." In popular usage the term canon refers to the collection of individual books that together comprise the Old and New Testaments. It is the complete list of books that is received by the church and is codified into what we call the Bible. The word *Bible* comes from the Greek word for "book." Strictly speaking the Bible is not a book, but a collection of sixty-six books. At least the classical Protestant Bible contains sixty-six books. The Roman Catholic Bible includes the Apocrypha and is therefore larger than sixty-six books. This points to the ongoing debate as to the precise nature of the canon. Rome and historic Protestantism disagree about the proper makeup of the biblical canon. Protestant creeds exclude the Apocrypha from the canon.

This disagreement about the Apocrypha points to the larger issue that surrounds the question of canon. How was the canon established? By whose authority? Is the canon closed to further additions? These and other questions attend the broader issue of the nature of the biblical canon.

One of the most important questions regarding the canon is the question of its historical compilation. Did the canon come into being by the fiat of the church? Was it already in existence in the primitive Christian community? Was the canon established by a special providence? Is it possible that certain books that made their way into the present canon should not have been included? Is it possible that books that were excluded should have been included?

We know that at least for a temporary period Martin Luther raised questions about the inclusion of the Epistle of James in the New Testament canon. That Luther once referred to

James as an "Epistle of Straw" or a "right strawy Epistle" is a matter of record. Critics of biblical inspiration have not grown weary of pointing to these comments of Luther to argue their case that Luther did not believe in the inspiration or infallibility of Scripture. This argument not only fails to do justice to Luther's repeated assertions of the divine authority of Scripture and their freedom from error, but more seriously it fails to make the proper distinction between the question of the nature of Scripture and the extent of Scripture. Luther was unambiguous in his conviction that all of Scripture is inspired and infallible. His question about James was not a question of the inspiration of Scripture but a question of whether James was in fact Scripture.

Though Luther did not challenge the infallibility of Scripture he most emphatically challenged the infallibility of the church. He allowed for the possibility that the church could err, even when the church ruled on the question of what books properly belonged in the canon. To see this issue more clearly we can refer to a distinction often made by Dr. John Gerstner. Gerstner distinguishes between the Roman Catholic view of the canon and the Protestant view of the canon in this manner:

> Roman Catholic view: The Bible is an infallible collection of infallible books.
> Protestant view: The Bible is a fallible collection of infallible books.

The distinction in view here refers to the Catholic Church's conviction that the canon of Scripture was declared infallibly by the church. On the other hand, the Protestant view is that the church's decision regarding what books make up the canon was a fallible decision. Being fallible means that it is possible that the church erred in its compilation of the books found in the present canon of Scripture.

When Gerstner makes this distinction he is neither asserting nor implying that the church indeed *did* err in its judgment of what properly belongs to the canon. His view is not designed to cast doubt on the canon but simply to guard against the idea of an infallible church. It is one thing to say that the church *could* have erred; it is another thing to say that the church *did* err.

Gerstner's formula has often been met with both consternation and sharp criticism in evangelical circles. It seems to indicate that he and those who agree with his assessment are undermining the authority of the Bible. But nothing could be further from the truth. Like Martin Luther and John Calvin before him, Gerstner has been an ardent defender of the infallibility and inerrancy of Scripture. His formula is merely designed to acknowledge that there was a historical selection process by which the church determined what books were really Scripture and what books were not Scripture. The point is that in this sifting or selection process the church sought to identify what books were actually to be regarded as Scripture.

It may be said that Rome has a certain "advantage" with respect to infallibility. Rome believes that the church is infallible as well as the Scripture. This infallibility extends not only to the question of canon formation but also to the question of biblical interpretation. To summarize, we can say that according to Rome we have an infallible Bible whose extent is decreed infallibly by the church and whose content is interpreted infallibly by the church. The Christian individual is still left in his own fallibility as he seeks to understand the infallible Bible as interpreted by the infallible church. No one is extending infallibility to the individual believer.

For the classic Protestant, though the individual believer has the right to the private interpretation of Scripture, it is clearly acknowledged that the individual is capable of misinterpreting the Bible. He has the ability to misinterpret Scripture, but never the right to do it. That is, with the right of private interpretation the responsibility of correct interpretation is also given. We never have the right to distort the teaching of Scripture. Both sides agree that the individual is fallible when seeking to understand the Scripture. Historic Protestantism limits the scope of infallibility to the Scriptures themselves. Church tradition and church creeds can err. Individual interpreters of Scripture can err. It is the Scriptures alone that are without error.

The New Testament Canon

Though it is clear that the church went through a selection or sorting process in establishing a formal list of the canonical books, this does not mean that there was no canon or rule prior to the decisions of church councils. The New Testament writings served as a functional canon from the beginning. Benjamin Breckinridge Warfield remarks:

> The church did not grow up by natural law: it was founded.
> And the authoritative teachers sent forth by Christ to found
> His church carried with them, as their most precious pos-

session, a body of divine Scriptures, which they imposed on the church that they founded as its code of law. No reader of the New Testament can need proof of this; on every page of that book is spread the evidence that from the very beginning the Old Testament was as cordially recognized as law by the Christian as by the Jew. The Christian church thus was never without a "Bible" or a "canon."[1]

Warfield's point that the church was founded calls attention to the fact that the church had a founder and a foundation. The founder was Christ. The foundation was the writings of the prophets and the apostles. In the image of the church as a building the metaphor views Christ as the chief cornerstone. He is not the foundation of the church. He is the founder. The foundation of the church is laid by Christ and in Christ. He is the Chief Cornerstone in which this foundation is laid. Again it is the prophets and the apostles who are called the foundation in the building metaphor.

The canon of the New Testament rests upon a "tradition." The term *tradition* is often viewed by a jaundiced eye among evangelicals. It suffers from the problem of guilt by association. In order to distance itself from the role played by tradition in Rome, zealous evangelicals face the danger of throwing out the baby with the bath water. The Reformation principle of *sola Scriptura* emphatically rejects the dual-source theory of Rome with respect to special revelation. At the fourth session of the Council of Trent, Rome declared that the truth of God is found both in the Scriptures and in the tradition of the church. The Reformers rejected this dual source and refused to elevate church tradition to such a high level.

Christ rebuked the Pharisees for supplanting the word of God with the traditions of men. This negative judgment of human tradition coupled with the aversion to the Roman Catholic view of tradition has inclined some evangelicals to reject tradition altogether. The danger in this is to miss the important role tradition plays within the scope of Scripture itself. Scripture does not reject all tradition. It repudiates the traditions of men, but affirms another tradition—the divine tradition. Paul, for example, frequently speaks of tradition in a positive sense. He speaks of that body of truth that was given over to the church by Christ and the apostles. This is the *paradosis*, the "giving over" of the truth of God.

The positive tradition of which Scripture speaks may be referred to as the apostolic tradition, which tradition played heavily on the formation of the canon. The church did not create a new tradition by the establishing of the canon. Indeed it is not really proper to speak of the establishing of the canon by the church. It is not the church that established the canon; it is the canon that established the church. The church did not establish the canon but recognized it and submitted to its rule.

At the heart of the canon question is the issue of apostolic authority. In the New Testament the apostle (*apostolos*) is "one who is sent." The office of the apostle carries with it the delegated authority of the One who sends or authorizes the apostle to speak in his behalf. The apostolic tradition begins with God the Father. The Father is the One who first commissioned an apostle. The first apostle in the New Testament is Christ himself as he is sent by the Father and speaks with the Father's delegated authority. It is to

Christ that the Father gives "all authority in heaven and on earth." The second apostle is the Holy Spirit, who is sent by both the Father and the Son. Next in line of delegated authority are the New Testament apostles such as Peter and Paul (and the rest).

In the patristic period of church history Irenaeus understood this linkage. In defending the apostles over against heretics, Irenaeus argued that to reject the apostles was to reject the One who sent them, namely Christ. To reject Christ is to reject the One who sent him, namely God the Father. Thus, for Irenaeus to reject the apostolic teaching was to reject God. At this point Irenaeus was merely echoing the words of Jesus when he said to his apostles that whoever received them received him and whoever rejected them rejected him.

It was the apostolic tradition that was codified in the formalization of the New Testament canon. The apostolic tradition was not limited to the writings of the apostles themselves exclusively. Rather the canon of Scripture contains the writings of the apostles and their *companions*. Again Warfield comments:

> Let it, however, be clearly understood that it was not exactly apostolic *authorship* which, in the estimation of the earliest churches, constituted a book or portion of the "canon." Apostolic authorship was, indeed, early confounded with canonicity. It was doubt as to the apostolic authorship of Hebrews, in the West, and of James and Jude, apparently, which underlies the slowness of the inclusion of these books in the "canon" of certain churches. But from the beginning it was not so. The principle of canonicity was not apostolic

authorship, but *imposition by the apostles as "law."* Hence Tertullian's name for the "canon" is *instrumentum;* and he speaks of the Old and New *Instrument* as we would of the Old and New Testament.[2]

That the church had a "functional canon" from the beginning is seen from the writings of the New Testament itself. Peter, in AD 68, refers to Paul's writings as being included among the "other Scriptures" (2 Peter 3:16). Paul also quotes from Luke's Gospel in 1 Timothy 5:18. From the earliest period of the postapostolic age the church fathers treated the New Testament writings as Scripture. Though the early fathers did not customarily use the word *Scripture,* they treated the apostolic writings with scriptural authority. Quotations taken from the writings of the New Testament and cited as authorities may be found in the writings of Clement, Ignatius, Polycarp, Papias, Justin Martyr, and others.

Toward the end of the second century Tatian's *Diatessaron* contained a harmony of the Gospels. The Muratorian canon (probably of the late second century) contained a list of New Testament books that perhaps was aimed to counter the false canon created by the heretic Marcion. Marcion's canon was a deliberate attempt to give an expurgated version of the New Testament to accommodate his negative view of the Old Testament God. Marcion's "New Testament" included the Gospel of Luke and ten of Paul's Epistles.

From the earliest period of her history it is clear that the vast majority of the books that are now contained in the New Testament canon were functioning as "canon" in the church. Some doubts were raised concerning a few of these books including Hebrews, James, 2 Peter, 2–3 John, Jude, and Revelation. These books lacked universal endorsement. It was not until the fourth century that the disputes were ended and the formal sanction of the entire New Testament canon was completed. Athanasius of Alexandria cited all 27 books in AD 367. In 363 the Council of Laodicea listed all of the present books except Revelation. The Third Council of Carthage in AD 397 included all of the present books in the canon.

During the debates in the early centuries certain criteria emerged by which books were determined to be canonical. These *notae canonicitatis* included (1) apostolic origin, (2) reception by the original churches, and (3) consistency with the undisputed core of canonical books. Apostolic origin included not only the books that were written by the apostles themselves but also those books that were authorized by the apostles. For example, the Gospel of Mark was seen as carrying the imprimatur of Peter, and the Gospel of Luke the sanction of Paul.

The reception of books by the original churches referred to the cultic use of these writings in the worship and teaching of the churches. The Latin word *recipere* was used in the Muratorian Canon to indicate that the church "received" the New Testament books.[3] Books that were excluded from the canon included such writings as the Didache, the Shepherd of Hermas, the Epistle of Barnabas, and First Clement. A study of these books quickly reveals their subcanonical status. There is a clear recognition, for example, in the writings of Clement that a line exists between apostolic and subapostolic authority.

Everett F. Harrison writes concerning these subcanonical books:

H. E. W. Turner notes that a measure of conflict might arise in the application of these criteria. A book might be widely received and appreciated and yet turn out to be unapostolic. Such was the case with the *Shepherd of Hermas*, which had to be excluded from use in public worship, but which was countenanced for purposes of private edification. This helps to explain the origin of a class of early Christian literature known as ecclesiastical, distinguished alike from canonical and from spurious writings, containing such works as the *Epistle of Clement* and the *Epistle of Barnabas*, as well as the *Shepherd of Hermas*.[4]

In addition to these books the church rejected a rash of spurious books that appeared as early as the second century known as apocryphal books. These books were often linked with the writings of the gnostic heretics who sought to usurp the authority that was vested in the New Testament apostles. The gnostics claimed to have a special elite knowledge (*gnosis*) that transcended the knowledge imparted by the apostles. At the same time they tried to gain apostolic credibility for their books by claiming they were written by the apostles themselves. This was an example of propaganda literature that sought to undermine the apostolic tradition. Origen said of these writings:

> The church receives only four gospels; heretics have many, such as the gospel of the Egyptians, the Gospel of Thomas, etc. These we read, that we may not seem to be ignorant to those who think they know something extraordinary, if they are acquainted with those things which are recorded in these books. Ambrose is credited with saying, "we read these that we may not seem ignorant; we read them, not that we receive

them, but that we may reject them; and may know what those things are, of which they make such a boast."[5]

The so-called apocryphal gospels abound with fanciful stories and heretical teaching. Some attempt to fill in details of the childhood years of Jesus. The Gospel of Thomas, for example, contains an account of frivolous miracles performed by the boy Jesus such as fashioning birds out of clay and then making them fly away.

The Old Testament Canon

The chief difference between the Roman Catholic canon and the Protestant canon is found with respect to the inclusion of the Old Testament Apocrypha. The Apocrypha (not to be confused with New Testament apocryphal writings) refers to a series of books composed during the intertestamental period. The Roman Catholic Church includes the Apocrypha and historic Protestantism excludes it. The Hebrew Scriptures are customarily referred to as "The Law, the Prophets, and the Writings." The issue focuses on the historical question of the extent of the Old Testament canon. Did the Jewish canon include the Apocrypha?

Frequently reference is made to the difference between the Palestinian canon and the Alexandrian canon. History indicates that the canon of Hellenized Jews of Alexandria included the Apocrypha but that the Hebrew Bible of the Palestinian canon excluded it. R. K. Harrison writes:

> In any discussion of the Old Testament canon it is of importance to distinguish between that of the Hebrew Bible and

its counterpart in other versions of Scripture. The degree of difference in the idea of a canon of sacred writings can be seen by reference on the one hand to the Samaritan version, in which only the Pentateuch was accorded canonicity, and on the other to the LXX, which included the writings known as the Apocrypha.[6]

The debate over the question of the Apocrypha is complex and ongoing. Some have argued that even in the Alexandrian canon the Apocrypha was accorded secondary status and was regarded as "deutero-canonical." This view is disputed by Roman Catholic scholars, who argue that the Apocrypha belonged to the original Jewish canon.

The Reformers excluded the Apocrypha because they were persuaded that it did not belong to the Hebrew canon recognized in Jesus' day. Francis Turretin remarks:

> The Jewish church, to which the oracles of God were committed (Rom. 3:2), never considered them as canonical, but held the same canon with us (as admitted by Josephus, *Against Apion*). . . . They are never quoted as canonical by Christ and the apostles like the others. And Christ, by dividing all the books of the Old Testament into three classes (the law, the Psalms and the prophets), clearly approves of the canon of the Jews and excludes from it those books which are not embraced in these classes. The Christian church for four hundred years recognized with us the same and no other canonical books. . . . The authors were neither prophets and inspired men, since they wrote after Malachi (the last of the prophets); nor were their books written in the Hebrew language (as those of the Old Testament), but in Greek. Hence Josephus acknowledges that those things which were writ-

ten by his people after the time of Artaxerxes were not equally credible and authoritative with those which preceded "on account of there not being an indisputable succession of prophets."[7]

Church and Canon

One of the great controversies of the Reformation centered on the relative authority of church and Scripture. It is often said that though *sola fide* was the material cause of the Reformation, *sola Scriptura* was its formal cause. Luther insisted that both popes and church councils could err. He rested his case for justification on the Scriptures alone. Rome countered by arguing that in a real sense the Scripture owed its authority to the authority of the church because it was the church that "created" the canon. This view was sharply criticized by Calvin:

Nothing, therefore, can be more absurd than the fiction, that the power of judging Scripture is in the church, and that on her nod its certainty depends. When the church receives it, and gives it the stamp of her authority, she does not make that authentic which was otherwise doubtful or controverted, but acknowledging it as the truth of God, she as in duty bound, shows her reverence by an unhesitating assent. As to the question, How shall we be persuaded that it came from God without recurring to a decree of the Church? It is just the same as if it were asked, How shall we learn to distinguish light from darkness, white from black, sweet from bitter? Scripture bears upon the face of it as clear evidence of its truth, as white and black do of their color, sweet and bitter of their taste.[8]

For Calvin the Bible is objectively the Word of God and derives its authority from him and not from the church. The church does not create Scripture but receives it (*recipimus*) and submits to an authority that is already there. Calvin knew nothing of a Bible that only "becomes" the Word of God after a church declaration or even after the Holy Spirit illumines it.

For the Reformers the Bible was "canon" as soon as it was written. The Word of God has inherent authority. The church is obliged to acknowledge that authority and to submit to it.

The Problem of Canon Reduction

The problem of canon reduction may manifest itself either in crude and blatant terms or in refined and subtle ways. The ancient heretic Marcion represented the crude form of such reduction by rejecting those portions of the New Testament that referred to the God of the Old Testament in a positive light. Marcion's antipathy to Yahweh controlled his selection of books to be included in his abridged version of the New Testament.

More modern forms of canon reduction are more refined and sometimes subtle. This form achieves a similar purpose by providing a canon within a canon. Since Albert Schweitzer's epic work, *The Quest of the Historical Jesus*, many subsequent attempts have been made to get to the "real" history of Jesus that underlies the work of the New Testament. The present form of the New Testament is viewed as the creation of the early church with redactions by editors who embellished the narrative history of Jesus. This attempt

53

to watch the grass grow from a distance of nearly two thousand years reaches its nadir in the contemporary work of the "Jesus Seminar."

Perhaps the most important work of canon reduction in the twentieth century was that undertaken by Rudolf Bultmann. Bultmann's program of "demythologizing" the New Testament was an attempt to rid the New Testament of its mythological husk to penetrate to the kernel of truth that is concealed by the husk. It was an attempt to reconstruct the original history as extrapolated from the *kerygma*. Bultmann declared:

> All this is the language of mythology, and the origin of the various themes can be easily traced in the contemporary mythology of Jewish Apocalyptic and in the redemption myths of Gnosticism. To this extent *the kerygma is incredible to modern man, for he is convinced that the mythical view of the world is obsolete.* We are therefore bound to ask whether, when we preach the Gospel today, we expect our converts to accept not only the Gospel message, but also the mythical view of the world in which it is set. If not, does the New Testament embody a truth which is quite independent of its mythical setting? If it does, theology must undertake the task of stripping the Kerygma from its mythical framework, of "demythologizing" it.[9]

Bultmann sets forth the task of freeing the timeless gospel from a time-bound mythical framework. He sought a theology of timelessness, a theology that would be relevant to the *hic et nunc*. He offers us a "here and now" canon, which reduces the original canon by the radical critical method of scissors and paste. For the gospel to be relevant for modern

man the interpreter must come to the text with a "prior understanding," a certain *vorverstandnis*, which Bultmann conve-
niently discovered in the philosophy of Martin Heidegger.

For modern persons to discover anything meaningful for
faith they must come to the text of Scripture asking the right
questions. These questions are formed by the insights
grasped via existential philosophy. For Bultmann, salvation
is not tied to the strata of history but is punctiliar. It occurs
not on the horizontal plane of time and space but comes to
us in a moment of decision, vertically from above.

In this schema the gospel must be rescued from the three-
storied universe of the biblical world view, which features
an earth that is situated beneath the heaven above and hell
below. Bultmann writes:

> *Man's knowledge and mastery of the world* have advanced to
> such an extent through science and technology that it is no
> longer possible for anyone seriously to hold the New Tes-
> tament view of the world—in fact, there is no one who does.
> What meaning, for instance, can we attach to such phrases
> in the creed as "descended into hell" or "ascended into
> heaven"? . . . It is impossible to use electric light and the
> wireless and to avail ourselves of modern medical and sur-
> gical discoveries, and at the same time to believe in the New
> Testament world of spirits and miracles. We may think we
> can manage it in our own lives, but to expect others to do
> so is to make the Christian faith unintelligible and unac-
> ceptable to the modern world.[10]

Here we find canon reduction with a vengeance.
G. C. Berkouwer once remarked about Bultmann's view
that theology could sink no lower. This sanguine view of

the matter reveals that Berkouwer was reading history through rose-colored glasses. He made this remark before the death-of-God movement in theology and the more recent Jesus Seminar wherein biblical criticism degenerated into biblical vandalism.

This shift in focus manifest in Bultmann displays a shift in attention to the matter of canon from the authenticity of specific books to the question of the authenticity of material within certain books that have been accorded canonical status. Bultmann's program attacked the *formal* nature of the canon by attacking various forms of literature found within the historic canon.

Normally the issues raised by higher criticism are seen as being chiefly issues of hermeneutics and not about canon. But the new hermeneutics are rife with implications for the canon. The canon is effectively reduced not by subtracting books of the Bible from a designated list but by excising the content of Scripture by a stroke of the hermeneutical pen. The hermeneutics of the Reformation featured the normative principle of grammatico-historical exegesis. But once the content of Scripture was wrenched out of its historical framework this norm was devastated.

The Reformed hermeneutic represented a commitment to seeking the "objective" meaning of the historical text. Bultmann eschewed this methodology arguing that objective interpretation of the Bible was not only not possible, but more importantly, not even desirable. From his vantage point all an objective reading of Scripture would gain us would be a gospel tied to an irrelevant mythological world view.

The crisis of canon today is a crisis of world view. It is the result of an ongoing struggle between naturalism and supernaturalism. The modern hermeneutic is an attempt to recover a naturalistic canon from the supernaturally conceived message of Scripture. All that smacks of anything supernatural is ruled out from the start. The new "canon" is the rigid canon of naturalism. Emil Brunner was correct when he observed early on that the real issue we face in this debate is a crisis of unbelief. Bultmannianism and post-Bultmannian theology are a monument to such unbelief where the "Christ of faith" has little to do with the Christ of history or the Christ of the New Testament.

Evangelical circles have not escaped modern forms of reductionism. The inerrancy controversy of the twentieth century was not merely a war between modernism and fundamentalism or between liberalism and orthodoxy. It cut to the core of professed Evangelicalism itself as professing evangelicals were sharply divided on the question.

A form of canon reduction arose within the ranks of evangelicals in sometimes subtle ways. Concepts of "limited inerrancy" and the "organic view of Scripture" effected a reduction in the normative function of Scripture. For example, the historic claim that the sacred Scriptures are the "only infallible rule of faith and practice" underwent a subtle change in some quarters. The new expression was articulated by the formula "The Bible is infallible only in matters of faith and practice." These formulae sound very much the same but mean two quite different things. To discriminate between them let us examine them more closely:

Premise A: The Bible is the only infallible rule of faith and practice.

> Premise B: The Bible is infallible only in matters of
> faith and practice.

In premise A the term "only" is restrictive with respect to norms. It declares that there is only one norm or rule that is infallible, namely the Bible. This indicates that the Bible as a whole and in all of its parts is an infallible rule or norm.

In premise B the term "only" is restrictive in quite a different sense. Here what is restricted is the scope of infallibility within the Bible. That is, only part of the Bible is infallible, namely that part of the Bible that speaks of matters regarding faith and practice. Here we have a canon that is reduced to that content of Scripture that deals with matters of doctrine and ethics. When the Bible speaks of other matters, such as history, for example, it may be fallible. This of course has a huge impact on the doctrines themselves, but that is often overlooked.

The second critical difference in these two formulae may be seen in their use of the phrase "faith and practice." In premise A the phrase "faith and practice" defines and delineates the life of the Christian and the life of the church. What else does the Christian or the church have besides faith and practice? Here faith and practice refer to the sum of Christian living. Premise A then means that we have a single infallible rule, which rule governs all of our life.

The function of the phrase "faith and practice" is quite different in premise B. Here faith and life are limits of the scope of biblical rule. It restricts biblical infallibility to certain portions of the Scripture that speak to faith and practice, thereby reducing the scope of canonical rule.

Canon Addition

The canon of Scripture is capable not only of being reduced but also of being augmented. A crass form of that would be accomplished simply by adding books to the list of canonical Scriptures. There are few if any people who are lobbying to add contemporary writings to the New Testament. Nevertheless we are living in a time in which countless claims of new revelations are being made. Neopentecostal theology often views messages delivered in tongues or the utterance of "prophecy" as new forms of revelation. Sometimes these revelations are described as true revelations but not necessarily normative for the church (despite their often containing information that might benefit the entire church). If indeed these are new revelations that have value to the church, we ask, why wouldn't they be added to the canon?

The claims of private new revelations are many. Pat Robertson routinely gets the "word of knowledge" on national television. God reveals specific illnesses of people who live in various parts of the nation as he prays. I have seen him say things like, "Someone in Topeka, Kansas, is right this moment being healed of a goiter." This is an astonishing thing. Here is a man hundreds of miles from the scene who is getting supernatural revelation of the healing of a specific disease in a specific city. What puzzles me is the restricted specificity of these revelations. The disease and the city are named, but never the name and address of the person being healed. Here the prophecy can be neither verified nor falsified.

Oral Roberts tells the nation that God has revealed to him that his life will be taken if he doesn't receive a large amount of money in donations. Robert Tilton promises his constituents that he will mail them a special message from God if they send in their donations. These, of course, are crude forms of modern claims to added revelation. How these claims are entertained by the credulous is a matter of consternation for me.

But it gets more subtle. We hear respected Christian leaders claiming that God has "spoken to them" and given specific guidance and instructions upon which they are duty-bound to act and obey. They are careful to note that this divine speech was not in audible form and there is a disclaimer that this is not a new "revelation." Yet the message which is "laid on the heart" is so clear and powerful that to disobey it is to disobey the voice of God. I am not speaking here of the work of the Holy Spirit by which he illumines the text of Scripture in such a sharp manner as to bring us under conviction or direct our paths. But here the Spirit works *in* the Word and *through* the Word. I am speaking of the speaking of the Spirit that men claim is working *apart* from the Word and in *addition* to the Word.

Though such claims are more often than not attended by the disclaimer that they are not revelation, the way they *function* is as revelation so that the distinction between them and *bona fide* revelation is, in actuality, a distinction without a difference.

The true canon of Scripture is the rule of God that contains the whole counsel of God, nothing less and nothing more. When we subtract from that counsel we are guilty of canon reductionism. Perhaps the most common practical subtraction in our time within the evangelical community is the subtraction of the Old Testament in general and the law of God in particular. The Reformation union of law and gospel has all but been destroyed in modern Evangelicalism. Luther and Calvin were not neonomians who sought to construct a novel form of legalism. They were fierce opponents of both legalism and antinomianism. They believed firmly, however, that all of Scripture is revelatory. In one sense the Reformation witnessed a rediscovery of the Old Testament. The Old Testament reveals the character of God. Though Calvin, for example, argued that certain portions of the Old Testament have been abrogated by their perfect fulfillment in Christ, nevertheless the law still has a salutary role to play in the Christian's life. Calvin's famous threefold use of the law defended this thesis.

Perhaps we are living in the most antinomian period in church history. It is a time when attention to the law of God is not considered all that important. This represents a pernicious form of canon reductionism. The very rule of God himself is removed from our consideration by it.

Canon and Providence

Though these are perilous times for the church with regard to the normative function of the Bible in our lives, we remain optimistic for the future. That optimism is grounded in our conviction of the providence of God. It was by his singular providence that the Bible was originally given under his superintendence and by his inspiration. It was also by his providence that the original books of the Bible were preserved and accorded the status of canon. It is in providence that we trust for the future of the church. The Westminster Confession of Faith declares: "As the providence of God doth, in general, reach to all creatures; so, after a most special manner, it taketh care of his church, and disposeth all things to the good thereof" (5.7).

That the canon was originally established by a historical selection process, undertaken by fallible human beings and fallible institutions, is no reason to exclude from our consideration the role of the providence of God in these affairs. Some in the Reformed tradition have pointed to a *providentia specialissima* (special providence) in this regard. Abraham Kuyper particularly referred to our ability to trace the course of providence in the establishment of the canon.[11] It is the invisible hand of providence in the history of the church along with the explicit promises of Scripture regarding the church and God's own Word that gives comfort to our souls as we rest in the confidence of the abiding work of that same providence.

3

THE CASE FOR INERRANCY:
A METHODOLOGICAL ANALYSIS

he church of the twentieth century not only demands an apologia for the authority of her sacred Scriptures but an apologia for the apologia. In these times not only an adequate defense of inerrancy is necessary, but such a defense needs to be defended. The reason for this proliferation of apologies is clear. Not only do we face the viewpoint of those who maintain that the Bible is full of errors and consequently no cogent case for its inspiration or infallibility *can* be made, but many who maintain a high view of Scripture contend that a rational defense of inerrancy *ought not* to be made even if it could be made.

The position of this essay is to maintain that not only can a defense of inerrancy be presented, but that such a defense *ought* to be made. The purpose of this paper is not to provide a comprehensive apology for the case for inerrancy but rather to provide a methodological framework for such a defense. This will involve a brief rehearsal and analysis of methodological options that are before us.

The Confessional Method

The confessional method may be defined as that method by which the Scriptures are confessed to be the Word of God (being inspired, trustworthy, reliable, etc.) and this is recognized by faith alone. No rational defense for infallibility or inerrancy is given. On the contrary this method eschews such a defense for introducing foreign rationalistic elements into a purely fideistic approach. A major exponent of this method would be G. C. Berkouwer of the Netherlands. In his two-volume work on Holy Scripture (part of the larger series, *Dogmatische Studiën*) Berkouwer celebrates the Scriptures as the Word of God, as being inspired, sufficient, trustworthy, etc., but shrinks from the notion of verbal inspiration or inerrancy. Berkouwer sees the doctrine of inerrancy and/or verbal inspiration as involving a formalistic view of Scripture that isolates itself from the "message" of the Scripture itself. He directs his critique primarily against Roman Catholic views (particularly those arising out of the modernist controversy at the turn of the century)[1] and against positions articulated by American fundamentalism of the same period. He sees verbal inspiration as a product of a post-Reformation quest for rational certainty. He warns of the danger of a speculatively constructed theory of inspiration that provides an a priori escape hatch from all uncertainty. He sees in this theory an intrusion of foreign, Aristotelian elements into the Christian faith.[2]

Berkouwer speaks of a "confidence" *(vertrouwen)* in the trustworthiness of Scripture that is inseparably related to the contents of the message.[3]

It can also be evident that in Scripture we are not dealing with a self-constructed benchmark to which we would cling simply because in this crisis of certainties we need a sure and unimpeachable point of orientation. An explanation of this sort has frequently been given, for example, when in confessing the authority of the Scriptures, one deemed there to be a Protestant parallel with the benchmark of Roman Catholic thought: the infallibility of the pope. The Protestant view of the authority of Scripture would then be explained in psychological terms—motivated by a desire for a tangible and immovable benchmark—and one would, to use an expression of Lessing, speak of a paper pope.[4]

H. Berkhof accurately traces the development of Berkouwer's method in terms of a method of *"correlatie."* This method of correlation can be traced throughout Berkouwer's *Dogmatische Studiën* and involves a decisive shift in Berkouwer's view of Scripture. Berkhof sees Berkouwer moving through three different stages of biblical views. The first stage involves a view of the "complete authority of Scripture." This stage (directed against the movement toward subjectivism of German theology) is detected in Berkouwer's earlier writings including his doctoral dissertation of 1932, *Geloof en Openbaring in de nieuwere duitse Theologie,* his book *Karl Barth* (1936), and especially his major volume of 1938, *Het Probleem der Schriftkritiek.* The second phase which Berkhof delineates is that one which emphasizes the "Redemptive Content of Scripture," which he sees beginning in 1949 and manifesting itself clearly in *Geloof in Volharding*. The third and final phase is what Berkhof calls the "existential tendency of Scripture."[5] In the third phase Berkouwer seeks to steer a course between subjectivism and objectivism in which the accent is found on the personal involvement of the believer with the life-transforming message of the Scripture. This approach, which Cornelius Van Til calls "activistic,"[6] seeks to avoid a "causal approach" to the Word of God that would build an apologetic from the perspective of the believer who responds to God *ex auditu verbi*.

The strength of the method of confession as advocated by Berkouwer consists in the following: (1) This method escapes the perjorative, emotive categories so often identified with fundamentalism and orthodoxy. It is "organic" and open-ended enough to escape the appellations of "rigid," "dogmatic," "obscurantis," etc. (2) This method takes seriously the human element of Scripture and allows for a thorough-going analysis of the cultural, linguistic, and historical framework of the Scripture. This method can make abundant use of higher critical tools of biblical studies without abandoning a confidence of the trustworthiness of Scripture. (3) This method is free from any charge of a "docetic" view of Scripture such as that leveled by Karl Barth against orthodoxy. (4) This method provides liberation from any need to define and redefine such terms as *inerrancy* or *infallibility*. The believer is freed from any need to "harmonize" difficult passages into a coherent, "systematic" form. Berkouwer is in no danger of being accused of holding to a "mechanical" or "dictation" theory of inspiration.

The weaknesses of this method include the following: (1) Berkouwer's method leaves us without a rational apologetic. His method never takes us away from fideism. Consequently the Christian has no better argument to offer the unbeliever than does the Muslim with his Koran. (2) Berkouwer's method leaves us no way to solve the subject-object dilemma and offers no escape from an arbitrary subjectivism. Van Til says:

> If Berkouwer thinks that an activistic pattern of thinking is a better means of expressing the doctrines of grace than the traditional one, he would oblige us by showing how he can, by using his method, avoid slipping into neo-orthodoxy altogether. So far, every time he uses the activist pattern of thought, his theology also becomes activist. When Berkouwer is most activist in his thinking he first starts off with causal thinking as though it were an intelligible way of thinking without the biblical pre-suppositions of creation and redemption, then he takes off into the realm of the unspeakable, the realm of praise without words, in order to finally return and speak of that realm in the language of causality.[7]

(3) Berkouwer's method leaves us without an answer to the crucial issue of our day concerning Scripture, namely the question of the *degree* of biblical trustworthiness. Is the Bible altogether and completely trustworthy? If so, then what is wrong with the categories of verbal inspiration and inerrancy? If not, then to what degree is the Bible *un*trustworthy? How do we deal with the biblical writers' claims for themselves? To what extent is the Bible the Word of God as well as the Word of man? Does God inspire error?

(4) Berkouwer's method is weak with respect to the one who is a spectator, namely, the unbeliever. Berkhof says: "I believe that the Scripture is less afraid of spectator-elements than Berkouwer."[8] To be sure, a believer's confidence in the biblical text is closely linked to the content of Scripture. We know that "faith comes by hearing and hearing from the Word of God." We respect the importance of faith that comes *ex auditu verbi*, but it seems that in the final analysis the only apologia Berkouwer leaves us is the plea *Tolle lege, tolle lege*.

The Presuppositional Method

The presuppositional method of apologetics follows closely the Dutch Calvinistic school that has been influenced heavily by Abraham Kuyper. The leading exponent of this methodology in the twentieth century has been Cornelius Van Til. Van Til's defense of Scripture follows closely his general method of apologetics, which is presuppositional. He says: "In fact it then appears that the argument for the Scripture as the infallible revelation of God is, to all intents and purposes, the same as the argument for the existence of God."[9] The starting point of all apologetics is clearly stated by Van Til: "A truly Protestant apologetic must therefore make its beginning from the presupposition that the triune God, Father, Son and Holy Spirit, speaks to him with absolute authority in Scripture."[10] Thus, according to Van Til, the proper method of defending the absolute authority of the Scripture is that method which incorporates the notion of the absolute authority of the Scripture in its foundational premise. Any method which does not proceed from the presuppositional basis of the absolute authority of the

Scripture involves a presupposition of human autonomy. Scripture must be taken as "self-attesting" if we are to avoid autonomous thinking.[11] Autonomous thinking or reasoning on "neutral ground" with unbelievers can only lead to conclusions that are at best "probably true." For the Christian to say that God's Word is "probably true" is to do violence to the integrity of God's self-revelation.

The presuppositional method of apologetics follows closely in the following way:

Premise A: The Bible is the infallible Word of God.
Premise B: The Bible attests to its own infallibility.
Premise C: The self-attestation of Scripture is an infallible attestation.
Conclusion: The Bible is the infallible Word of God.

Here we have a line of reasoning where the conclusion is explicitly stated in the opening premise. This approach has been and may fairly be called circular reasoning. The classical problem with circular reasoning is that it "begs the question."

Circular definitions are a rather obvious instance of question begging. In its full-blown maturity question begging can go on for volumes, even through whole systems of thought. As can be guessed, the mature fallacy is not easy to handle. There it is, big as the universe (in Hegel, for example), but just how it operates is hard to show in a simple instance.[12]

Van Til and others within the presuppositional school are not particularly bothered by the circularity of their approach.[13] Van Til, of course, recognizes circularity and goes on at great length to defend it. He maintains that all reasoning is circular in the final analysis. He says:

> To admit one's own presuppositions and to point out the presuppositions of others is therefore to maintain that all reasoning is, in the nature of the case, *circular reasoning.* The starting point, the method, and the conclusions are always involved in one another.[14]

Van Til has written extensively in an attempt to show that non-Christian presuppositional thinking is self-destructive. He maintains that any presupposition apart from the Christian one leads inevitably to irrationalism.[15] Only if one begins with the existence of God can reason be ultimately rational and coherent and empirical data be intelligible.

That Christianity alone provides an ultimately coherent worldview is not in dispute among Christian thinkers. That the presupposition of autonomy will lead inevitably to the denial of theism is not in dispute. That there is no higher authority possible than the testimony of God is not in dispute. That all men *ought* to recognize the Scripture as being the Word of God is not in dispute. That a Christian cannot abandon his conviction of the existence of God when he enters into debate with the unbeliever is not in dispute. That all reasoning is ultimately circular in the sense that conclusions are inseparably related to presuppositions is not in dispute. What is in dispute is the form of argument for Scripture.

When the classical method argues from historical reliability to infallibility, the existence of God is presupposed in a certain sense. (That is, the category of history has no meaningful basis apart from the existence of God.) But the argument is not explicitly circular. The progression is from general reliability to infallibility, not infallibility to infallibility. The issue is, of course, the issue of common ground. If we are to choose between two possible presuppositions, namely the existence of God or the autonomy of man, then by all means let us choose the former! But this is a false dilemma involving the either/or informal fallacy when there is in fact a *tertium quid* (self-consciousness). If the presupposition of the existence of God leads inevitably to the affirmation of the existence of God because it begins there and the presupposition of autonomy ends in autonomy (excluding God) because it begins there, how do we decide which presupposition to begin with? This leaves us with a choice between presuppositions that can only be made by pure subjectivism which is a pre-pre-supposition. To avoid this impasse of subjectivism classical apologists have sought a *tertium quid* that would provide a point of contact with the unbeliever: a presupposition shared by all. This presupposition which is first in the order of knowing, though not first in the order of being, is self-consciousness. By working with this presupposition, apologists have been able to reason *directly* rather than indirectly to the existence of God and the infallibility of Scripture. Though unbelievers may *assume* autonomy along with self-consciousness, the notion of autonomy is not analytically contained in the premise of self-consciousness. Apologists can and have shown that self-consciousness does not lead to or demand autonomy and that autonomy is a false assumption.

The strengths of the presuppositional method involve the exposure of the existence and poverty of pagan presuppositions. In Herman Dooyeweerd's categories autonomy has been exposed as a "pretense." Van Til's method is rich in its

71

critique-value of alternate systems of truth. His method exerts a restraining influence on those who would exalt reason to the primary place in order of *being* rather than knowing. He forces us to be careful about viewing epistemological systems such as rationalism or empiricism as being more authoritative than revelation.

The weaknesses of this method are focused in its dependence upon circularity in argument. The clear and present danger of this approach is subjectivism. As Benjamin Breckinridge Warfield detected a strong element of mysticism and subjectivism in Kuyper, so not a few contemporary evangelical scholars detect these elements in Van Til. The debate is an intermural one between men who agree as to the nature of Scripture but differ with respect to apologetic methodology. The debate continues as indicated in the compilation of essays found in Van Til's festschrift, *Jerusalem and Athens*.

The Classical Method

The classical approach to the defense of Scripture is one that concerns itself with both deduction and induction, external and internal evidence. The approach proceeds on the basis of a progression from the premise of basic or general trustworthiness of Scripture to the conclusion of inerrancy or infallibility. The reasoning proceeds as follows:

Premise A: The Bible is a basically reliable and trustworthy document.

Premise B: On the basis of this reliable document we have sufficient evidence to believe confidently that Jesus Christ is the Son of God.

Premise C: Jesus Christ being the Son of God is an infallible authority.

Premise D: Jesus Christ teaches that the Bible is more than generally trustworthy: it is the very Word of God.

Premise E: That the word, in that it comes from God, is utterly trustworthy because God is utterly trustworthy.

Conclusion: On the basis of the infallible authority of Jesus Christ, the Church believes the Bible to be utterly trustworthy, i.e., infallible.

It is important to note at this point that this method does not involve circular reasoning. Circular reasoning occurs when the conclusion is already present in the first premise. The argument itself is not an infallible argument as each premise involves matters of inductive or deductive reasoning by fallible rational creatures. There is neither a formal a priori assumption nor a subjective leap of faith in the method. Rather, the method is involved with careful historical, empirical investigation as well as with logical inferences.

Premise A. The argument, of course, stands or falls on the basis of this premise. If the biblical documents are not at least basically trustworthy then we have no historical basis for knowledge of Jesus at all. Without a reliable historical witness to Jesus the Christian faith would be reduced to an esoteric-gnostic religion. That the Bultmannian approach to faith has been called neognostic is inseparably related to its unhistorical methodology.

It is not within the scope of this essay to give a detailed defense of the general reliability of the biblical documents. Such a defense, at this point in history, should not be necessary in light of the overwhelming abundance of evidence and testimony confirming the historical reliability of the Scripture.[16] Only the most radical higher critics would deny the premise of basic or general reliability. One testimony, however, will be added. Consider the following passage from a joint statement issued by William Foxwell Albright, the dean of twentieth-century archaeologists, and C. S. Mann:

> For much too long a time the course of New Testament scholarship has been dictated by theological, quasi-theological, and philosophical presuppositions. In far too many cases commentaries on NT books have neglected such basic requirements as up-to-date historical and philological analysis of the text itself. In many ways this preoccupation with theological and metaphysical interpretation is the unacknowledged child of Hegelianism. To this should be added the continuing and baleful influence of Schleiermacher and his successors on the whole treatment of historical material. The result has often been steadfast refusal to take seriously the findings of archaeological and linguistic research. We believe that there is less and less excuse for the resulting confusion in this latter half of the twentieth century.
>
> Closely allied with these presuppositions is the ever present fog of existentialism, casting ghostly shadows over an already confused landscape. Existentialism as a method of interpreting the New Testament is based upon a whole series of undemonstrable postulates of Platonic, Neo-Platonic, left-wing scholastic, and relativistic origins. So anti-historical is this approach that it fascinates speculative minds which prefer clichés to factual data, and shifting ideology to empirical research and logical demonstration.[17]

That the case for the infallibility of Scripture rests on a premise that can only be established on the inductive basis of historical-empirical evidence should not be a problem to the Christian. It is on the historical-empirical plane that our redemption has been accomplished. The biblical witnesses are "eye" witnesses. If the eye witnesses are not reliable we are left with a subjectivistic arbitrary claim of unconditional importance of Jesus of Nazareth. If the Christian faith is indeed established on an historical foundation then it is essential that we have a reliable knowledge of the history. Without it, the subject-object polarity is reduced to one pole, namely the former.[18]

The basic reliability of the biblical witnesses provides a crucial point of contact for the Christian believer engaged in apologetics. Without it we must opt for fideism.

Premise B. If the biblical data concerning the person and work of Christ is reliable, we have sufficient evidence for any reasonable man to come to the conclusion that Jesus of Nazareth is God Incarnate. Again, it is beyond the scope of this essay to demonstrate that the New Testament does in fact clearly manifest the deity of Christ. I am aware, of course, that many people have indeed read the New Testament and have not been persuaded of the truth of its claims about Jesus. Many have endeavored to explain this by pointing to the sinful disposition of natural man that makes it impossible for him to acquiesce in the biblical claims without experiencing the internal testimony of the Holy Spirit. Unfortunately, we are often left with the impression that the biblical data, apart from the internal testimony, is insufficient to provide a rational-evidential basis for faith in Christ and that the Holy Spirit either provides new internal evidence for the believer that is unavailable to all, or that he gives the Christian the ability to leap over the evidence (being either insufficient or contrary) by an act of faith. Such a view of the internal testimony of the Spirit would involve a serious distortion of its classical meaning. For example, John Calvin points out:

> Let it therefore be held as fixed, that those who are inwardly taught by the Holy Spirit acquiesce implicitly in Scripture; that Scripture, carrying its own evidence along with it, deigns not to submit to proofs and arguments, but owes the full conviction with which we ought to receive it to the testimony of the Spirit.[19]

Again Calvin says:

> If then, we would consult most effectually for our consciences, and save them from being driven about in a whirl of uncertainty, from wavering, and even stumbling at the smallest obstacle, our conviction of the truth of Scripture must be derived from a higher source than human conjectures, judgments, or reason; namely, the secret testimony of the Spirit. It is true, indeed, that if we choose to proceed in the way of argument, it is easy to establish, by evidence of various kinds, that if there is a God in heaven, the Law, the Prophesies, and the Gospel proceeded from him. Nay, although learned men, and men of the greatest talent, should take the opposite side, summoning and ostentatiously displaying all the powers of their genius in the discussion, if they are not possessed of shameless effrontery, they will be compelled to confess that the Scripture exhibits clear evidence of its being spoken by God, and consequently, of its containing his heavenly doctrine.[20]

Thus, for Calvin, the testimony of the Spirit does not cause men to *acquiesce* contrary to the evidence but into the evidence of Scripture. The evidence of the Scripture for the deity of Christ is compelling. To refuse to acknowledge what is plainly manifest must be motivated by a sinful disposition that refuses to submit to what is plainly evident. If the biblical documents are a reliable historical source of information and their testimony of Jesus' activity is reliable we are left with no rational alternative to a bold declaration of his deity. If in fact he performed miracles, raised people from the dead, walked on water, was himself victorious over the grave, and claimed to be God, who can gainsay that claim?

Premise C. The content and ramifications of this premise are so crucial to the whole argument and so far-reaching that they are the subject of a complete essay in *God's Inerrant Word,* a symposium edited by John Warwick Montgomery. Rather than a detailed reiteration of the whole matter, I will touch lightly on the issues involved. The basic question raised in premise C is not the fact of Jesus' authority but the *scope* of it. It is fair to assume a consensus among Christians that Jesus Christ is the supreme authority of the church. This is acknowledged not only by Protestantism but by the Roman Catholic Church as well. Where papal authority is maintained at a human level of primacy it is still viewed as being a derived authority from the authority of Christ.

A classical point of dispute between Protestant christology and Roman Catholic christology has to do with the issue of the scope of Christ's knowledge. In Roman Catholic thought the infallibility of Christ is inseparably related to his omniscience. That is, because of the hypostatic union of divine and human natures Jesus' infallibility is rooted in the omniscience of the divine nature which exists in perfect unity with the human nature. This approach to Jesus' infallibility has been sharply criticized by Protestant theologians as being docetic, monophysite, and eutychian inasmuch as it involves a violation of Chalcedonian christology by confusing or mixing the two natures. The issue centers on the exegesis of Mark 13:32. In this text Jesus claims ignorance concerning the day and the hour of his coming. Traditional Roman Catholic exegesis has maintained that this text could not possibly reflect a limitation of the knowledge of Jesus. This view was made popular by Thomas Aquinas, who provided a kind of "accommodation theory" to avoid the inference of limited knowledge. Aquinas maintained that Christ did in fact know the day and the hour but the knowledge was incommunicable.[21] This view reflected the earlier exegesis of Gregory I and was ratified by a decree of 1918.[22] This accommodation view preserves the notion of an infallible Jesus but only by raising serious question about the *integrity* of Jesus.

Protestant christology has traditionally maintained that, touching Christ's human nature (which can be distinguished from though not separated from the divine nature), he had limited knowledge and in fact did not know the time of his parousia. Thus the issue for Protestantism is not, was the human Jesus *omniscient*, but was he *infallible?*

In recent times, it has been fashionable among Protestant thinkers to deny both omniscience and infallibility in Jesus. C. H. Dodd comments: "We need not doubt that Jesus, as He is represented, shared the views of His contemporaries regarding the authorship of books in the Old

Testament, or the phenomena of 'demon-possession'—
views which we could not accept without violence to our
sense of truth."[23] Emil Brunner confesses that Jesus shared
the high view of Scripture of his Jewish contemporaries:
"The Scriptures are to Him the revelation of God."[24] Yet
Brunner has no problem criticizing Jesus' understanding
and use of the Old Testament, saying that "the Bible is full
of errors, contradictions, erroneous opinions concerning all
kinds of human, natural, historical situations."[25]

Such attitudes toward the authority of the historical Jesus
are justified by seeing a limitation to the knowledge of Jesus
as part of his culturally conditioned humanness. Jesus could
no more be expected to know that Moses did not write the
Pentateuch than he could be expected to know the world
was round. Being human, he participated in knowledge-
gaps and erroneous views of the Old Testament common to
his day.

This approach to the knowledge and authority of Jesus
raises even more serious questions than the Roman Catholic
view. Not only does this impugn the integrity of Jesus' understanding of the relationship of the Old Testament Scriptures
to his own mission and identity,[26] but it casts a shadow over
his sinlessness. *Jesus does not have to be omniscient to be infallible. But he must be infallible to be sinless.* That is to say, if
Jesus, claiming to be sent from God and invoking the authority of God in his teaching errs in that teaching, he is guilty
of sin. The one who claims to be the truth cannot err and
be consistent with that claim. Anyone claiming absolute
authority in his teaching must be absolutely trustworthy in
what he teaches in order to merit absolute authority. In light

of his claims, Jesus cannot plead "invincible ignorance" as an excuse for error.

James Orr summarized the matter as follows:

> Does this acknowledged limitation of the human knowledge of Christ, and ignorance of earthly science, imply *error* on the part of Jesus? This is a position which must as strongly be contested. Ignorance is not error, nor does the one thing necessarily imply the other. That Jesus should use the language of His time on things indifferent, where no judgment or pronouncement of His own was involved, is readily understood; that He should be the victim of illusion, or false judgment, on any subject on which He was called to pronounce, is a perilous assertion. If the matter be carefully considered, it may be felt that even sinlessness is hardly compatible with liability of the judgment to error. False judgment, where moral questions are involved, can hardly fail to issue in wrong action.[27]

Premise D. Jesus' view of Scripture is not a hotly disputed issue. This question has been discussed in *God's Inerrant Word* both by John Frame in his essay on the *autopiste* and by Clark Pinnock in his paper on the authority of Christ. A multitude of writers have demonstrated clearly that Jesus held a very high view of Scripture. In addition to Dodd and Brunner (cited earlier), we could mention the work of John Murray, E. J. Young, Benjamin Breckinridge Warfield, James Orr, Roger Nicole, J. I. Packer, Clark Pinnock, and a host of other scholars who have demonstrated the high view of Scripture held by Jesus.

To be sure, questions have arisen concerning Jesus' view of Scripture, especially in light of Jesus' teaching in the Ser-

mon on the Mount vis-à-vis the Old Testament. Joachim
Jeremias maintains that Jesus exercises a positive criticism
of the Old Testament law by repealing the Mosaic permission for divorce and implicitly by "criticizing the Torah primarily by omitting elements of it."[28] Nevertheless Jeremias
agrees that to charge Jesus with antinomianism is a misinterpretation: "Jesus is not concerned with destroying the law
but with filling it to its full eschatological measure."[29]
Though Jeremias sees a radical rejection by Jesus of the Rab-
binic Halakah (the oral tradition), the same kind of attitude
is not demonstrated toward the Torah.

> Jesus lived in the Old Testament. His sayings are incom-
> prehensible unless we recognize this. His last word, accord-
> ing to Mark, was the beginning of Psalm 22, prayed in his
> Aramaic mother tongue (Mark 15:34). He was particularly
> fond of the prophet Isaiah, and above all of the promises
> and statements about the servant of God in Deutero-Isaiah.
> The apocalyptic sayings of Daniel were also extremely sig-
> nificant for him. Numerically, literal and free quotations
> from the Psalter predominate on the lips of Jesus, and this
> was evidently his prayer book. The twelve prophets are also
> quoted frequently, and there are repeated allusions to the
> prophet Jeremiah. The numerous references to the Penta-
> teuch, in which Jesus found inscribed the basic norms of the
> will of God, occur especially in the controversy sayings.[30]

That Jesus' view of Scripture was high is beyond dispute.
That he regarded the Scriptures as being utterly trustworthy can be seen from the following examples summarized
by J. I. Packer:

There is no lack of evidence for our Lord's attitude to the Old Testament. He prefaces with his regular formula of solemn assertion ("Verily [amen] I say unto you") the following emphatic assurance: "till heaven and earth pass, one jot or one tittle shall in no wise pass from the law." He quotes Gn. 2:24—in its context a comment passed by Adam or (more likely) the narrator—as an utterance of God: "have ye not read, that he which made them at the beginning . . . said . . . ?" He treats argument from Scripture as having clinching force. When he says "it is written," that is final. There is no appeal against Scripture, for "the Scripture cannot be broken." God's Word holds good forever.[31]

Thus, even a cursory view of Jesus' use of Scripture in debate, discussion, and rebuke of his own disciples, added to an examination of Jesus' own submission to the authority of Scripture, makes clear that the formula *Sacra Scriptura est Verbum Dei* was as vital for him as it would be for the Reformers. That Jesus considered and treated the Old Testament as of divine authority is clear.[32]

Premise E. If God is utterly trustworthy, then his Word carries the trustworthiness of himself. This premise has been subjected to rigorous criticism. What is at issue of course is not that God himself is utterly trustworthy or infallible but that a book which comes to us through human means can bear that degree of trustworthiness. The church has recognized that although the Bible is the *vox Dei* or the *Verbum Dei*, it is at the same time, the word of man. The controversial confessional statement issued by the United Presbyterian Church in the U.S.A. states the matter as follows:

The Scriptures, given under the guidance of the Holy Spirit,
are nevertheless the words of men, conditioned by the language, thought forms, and literary fashions of the places and
times at which they were written. They reflect views of life,
history, and cosmos which were then current. The church,
therefore, has an obligation to approach the Scriptures with
literary and historical understanding.[33]

The confession elsewhere calls the Bible the "Word of God
written." Here the Scriptures are viewed as being both the
Word of God and the word of man. The question arises then,
Can the Bible, being the word of man, be utterly trustworthy in light of the propensity of man for error and human
fallibility? Can we take the proverbial maxim "To err is
human" and treat it as a tautology which can be reversed to
say "To be human is to err"? Though we grant that God is
incapable of error must we also admit that man is incapable
of being free from error?

Karl Barth has described the view of verbal inspiration
or inerrancy of the Bible as one that involves a kind of biblical docetism. He draws the conclusion that the Bible is fallible because humans are fallible and the Bible is a human
document.

The men whom we hear as witnesses speak as fallible, erring
men like ourselves. What they say, and what we read as their
word, can of itself lay claim to be the word of God, but never
sustain that claim. We can read and try to assess their word
as a purely human word. It can be subjected to all kinds of
immanent criticism, not only in respect of its philosophical,
historical and ethical content, but even of its religious and
theological. We can establish lacunae, inconsistencies and

over-emphases. We may be alienated by a figure like that of Moses. We may quarrel with James or with Paul. We may have to admit that we can make little or nothing of large tracts of the Bible, as is often the case with the records of other men. We can take offence at the Bible.[34]

Again Barth adds:

> The prophets and apostles as such, even in their office, even in their function as witnesses, even in the act of writing down their witness, were real, historical men as we are, and therefore sinful in their action, and capable and actually guilty of error in their spoken and written word.[35]

For Barth, failure to confess such errors and contradictions would be to be guilty of docetism.[36] Barth draws a parallel between biblical docetism and christological docetism, which is indeed a strange one. Christological docetism involves a failure to take the human nature of Christ seriously. As the ancient docetists were scandalized by the notion of incarnation, so orthodox thinkers are scandalized by biblical fallibility. The docetists were guilty of allowing the deity of Christ to swallow up his humanity and leave us with only an "apparent" or "phantom" human nature. So, according to Barth, orthodoxy has allowed the human aspect of the Bible to be swallowed up by the divine when it fails to leave room for human error.

This is a strange analogy indeed! Barth misses the issue completely and produces an argument so fallacious that one wonders how anyone can take it seriously. If we push the analogy we would be forced to ask if Christ could be sinless and still be a man? If being human demands error, is a man not a man when he speaks the truth? The term *fallible* describes an *ability*, not an *act*. To say that men are fallible is to say they are *capable* of error, not that they *must* err or that they *always* err. In theological terms, Christ's sinlessness no more cancels his humanity than does inerrancy cancel the biblical writers' humanity.

What is at issue is not the question whether or not human beings *can* err. What is at issue is the question whether or not God inspires error or the Holy Spirit guides into error. When orthodoxy confesses the infallibility of Scripture it is not confessing anything about the intrinsic infallibility of men. Rather the confession rests its confidence on the integrity of God. On numerous occasions I have queried several biblical and theological scholars in the following manner: "Do you maintain the inerrancy of Scripture?"

"No."

"Do you believe the Bible to be the inspired Word of God?"

"Yes."

"Do you think God inspires error?"

"No."

"Is all of the Bible inspired by God?"

"Yes."

"Is the Bible errant?"

"No!"

"Is it inerrant?"

"No!"

At that point I usually acquire an Excedrin headache. The above dialogue is not a construction of my fancy but a verbatim reproduction of a dialogue I have encountered on numerous occasions. To be sure, there are numerous ways of setting up false dilemmas and committing the either/or informal fallacy when there may be a *tertium quid*. But where is the *tertium quid* between errancy and inerrancy? *In*errancy is a category that incorporates everything outside of the category of errancy. To affirm or deny both categories is to be involved in logical absurdity. Logical absurdity, however, does not bother some thinkers who see in absurdity the hallmark of truth.

Unless we want to join the ranks of the absurd, or unless we confess that God inspires error and join the ranks of the impious, or unless we confess that the Bible as a whole is not inspired, then we are forced by what Martin Luther called "resistless logic" to the conclusion that the Bible is inerrant.

The "resistless logic" of which Luther speaks is not a logic of isolated abstract speculations. It is a logic that is driven to a conclusion drawn from the premise of the integrity of Christ. The Bible is not claimed to be inerrant because of confidence in human ability. Rather the claim rests upon the foundation of the integrity of Christ. As Martin Kähler pointed out in the nineteenth century: "We do not believe in Christ because we believe in the Bible, but we believe in the Bible because we believe in Christ."[37]

That orthodoxy moves from confidence in Christ's infallibility to confidence in the Scripture has not always been clearly understood. For example, Bernard Zylstra has criticized "orthodox theological circles" for viewing the Bible as the Word of God *because* it contains "propositional truth."[38] This, however, is a caricature in that it reverses the order. Orthodoxy does not believe the Bible to be the Word of God because it contains propositional truth—but believes the Bible to contain propositional *truth* because it is the Word of God.

It is important to add at this point that terms like *inerrant* or *infallible* must gain their content from a biblical understanding of truth. The protests of Berkouwer and others against "inerrancy" are often rightly directed against an imposition on the biblical text of a notion of truth that is foreign to the Bible itself. Much unfair criticism has been leveled at orthodox thinkers at this point inasmuch as many have labored to clarify the notion of inerrancy along biblical lines.

The late E. J. Young provides us with an excellent treatment of the question of the meaning of inerrancy and infallibility. He says:

> In present discussions of the Bible, both the words infallibility and inerrancy are often used without attempt at definition. The result is that much confusion has adhered and does adhere to current discussions of inspiration. There is not much point in talking of an infallible and inerrant Bible, unless we know what the words mean.[39]

Young goes on to define the terms by saying:

> By the term infallible as applied to the Bible, we mean simply that the Scripture possesses an indefectible authority. As our Lord himself said "it cannot be broken" (John 10:35). It can never fail in its judgments and statements. All that it teaches is of unimpeachable, absolute authority, and cannot be contravened, contradicted, or gainsaid. Scripture is unfailing, incapable of proving false, erroneous, or mistaken.[40]

He defines the term *inerrant* in similar categories: "By this word we mean that the Scriptures possess the quality of freedom from error. They are exempt from the liability to mistake, incapable of error. In all their teaching they are in perfect accord with the truth."[41]

Thus for Young, terms like *infallible* and *inerrant* are terms inseparably related to the notion of *truth*. To confess inerrancy is to confess the utter truthfulness of the Scripture. At this point Young, like Warfield before him and Berkouwer after him, warns against imposing an a priori notion of truth upon the Scripture which is at variance with the Bible's own view of truth. If the biblical writers and/or Jesus claimed "truth" for their writings we should test their claim by an analysis of their writings in terms of consistency to their own view of truth.

Young demonstrates that within the context of a biblical view of truth there is room for crudity and roughness of literary style, including improper grammatical structure, variations of parallel accounts of events, discourses, etc., but not room for contradiction or deception. Phenomenological, anthropomorphical, hyperbolic, etc. forms of language do not negate or falsify truth.

Hans Küng has commented on the relationship of the word *infallible* to the notion of deception:

> Bearing in mind the root of the word *infallibilitas (fallere—* put wrong, make a false step, lead into error, deceive, delude), I later translated *infallibilitas* more precisely and perhaps also more felicitously as "indeceivability" (*Untrüglichkeit*), which certainly has a more general meaning. *Infallibilitas* can then be understood as a sharing in the truth of God himself who,

according to Vatican I, "can neither deceive nor be deceived" (*Deus revelans, qui nec falli nec fallere potest*—DS 3008). *Infallibilitas* would then mean being free from what is deceptive, from lying and fraud.[42]

Küng's definition of infallibility drawn by etymological derivation and customary usage within the Roman Catholic tradition is not far removed from the New Testament concept of "truth."

Rudolf Bultmann properly analyzes the New Testament meaning of *alētheia* in his article on that term in Gerhard Kittel's *Wörterbuch.* Truth in the New Testament is that which has "certainty and force," which is a "valid norm," "genuine," "proper," and "honest." Bultmann also indicates that *alētheia* is "that on which one can rely." The truth involves sincerity and honesty and is concerned with the "real state of affairs."[43]

When we confess that the Scriptures are inerrant and infallible we mean that they are *true* according to the categories mentioned above.

In summary, the Christian's case for infallibility rests in the reliable trustworthiness of the biblical documents which provide knowledge of the infallible Christ. The authority we give to Scripture ought to be no more and no less than that given to it by Christ. The church cannot submit to the authority of Christ without at the same time submitting to the authority of the Scripture. The apologist of the twentieth century must echo the argument of Irenaeus against the gnostics of his day:

If anyone does not agree with them [the apostles] he despises the companions of the Lord himself—he even despises the Father, and he is self-condemned, resisting and refusing his own salvation, as all the heretics do. . . . The apostles, being disciples of the truth, are apart from every lie. For a lie has no fellowship with the truth, anymore than light with darkness, but the presence of one excludes the other.[44]

4

THE INTERNAL TESTIMONY
OF THE HOLY SPIRIT

estimonium Spiritus Sancti internum. This Reformation slogan, indicating the internal testimony of the Holy Spirit, has become increasingly important as the church wrestles with the question of the integrity of Holy Writ. As we face a crisis of confidence in the authority and reliability of the apostolic deposit of faith we are drawn repeatedly into deep consideration of the relationship of Word and Spirit. The *testimonium* represents but one facet, albeit a vital facet, of this complex relationship of Word and Spirit.

The Holy Spirit is related to Scripture in many ways. Some of the more significant dimensions of the Spirit's work vis-à-vis Scripture include inspiration, illumination, application (conviction), and the *testimonium*.

Inspiration concerns the role of the Spirit in initiating and superintending Word revelation. The *theopneustos* of

2 Timothy 3:16 points to the divine origin of Holy Scripture as God "breathes out," or *inspires*, his Word.[1] *Illumination* concerns the Spirit's work in assisting the reader to achieve clarity in understanding the content of the Word. It is the Spirit who "searches" the deep things of God and works to assist our naturally carnal minds to understand spiritual things (1 Cor. 2:10, 14). *Application* refers to the work of the Spirit in applying the content of the Scripture to the life of the believer. A special type of application is conviction, which refers to the Spirit's work of bringing an awareness of sin to the conscience of the individual and a subsequent spirit of penitence to the heart of the convicted.

In all of these activities the Spirit is linked to the Word. The Spirit is not divorced from the Word in such a way as to reduce revelation to an exercise in subjectivism. The Spirit works *with* the Word *(cum verbo)* and *through* the Word *(per verbum)*, not *without* or apart from the Word *(sine verbo)*.[2]

How does the *testimonium* differ from the other facets of the Word and Spirit mentioned above? The uniqueness of the *testimonium* is found in its focus on the question of *certainty*. The Spirit in his internal testimony works to confirm the reliability of Scripture, giving us certainty that the Bible is the Word of God. Thus it has been in the arena of apologetics that the *testimonium* has received much attention.

The *Testimonium* in Calvin

John Calvin is usually credited with developing and giving the clearest expression to the Reformation principle of the *testimonium*. He treats this question in the early parts of his *Institutes of the Christian Religion* and in his *Letter to Sado-*

let. Controversy over interpreting Calvin's view of the *testimonium* has engendered some debate, particularly with respect to issues involving apologetics and most particularly with respect to methodological questions regarding the defense of biblical infallibility.[3]

In chapter 7 of the *Institutes* Calvin sets forth his doctrine of the *testimonium.* He divides his treatment into five sections.

In section 1 Calvin deals with the foundation of certainty, whether it is from men or from God. In full view here is the issue of whether or not the authority of Scripture rests on the prior authority of the church. He writes:

> A most pernicious error has very generally prevailed—viz.
> that Scripture is of importance only insofar as conceded to
> it by the suffrage of the Church; as if that eternal and invi-
> olable truth of God could depend on the will of men. With
> great insult to the Holy Spirit, it is asked, who can assure us
> that the Scriptures proceeded from God; who can guaran-
> tee that they have come down safe and unimpaired to our
> times; who can persuade us that this book is to be received
> with reverence, and that one expunged from the list; did not
> the Church regulate all these things with certainty? On the
> determination of the Church, therefore, it is said, depend
> both the reverence which is due to Scripture and the books
> which are to be admitted into the canon.[4]

Here Calvin obviously had Rome in mind as he wrestled with the question of the ultimate basis for *reverence* for Scripture and with the issue of canon. Rome consistently appealed to the church's role in the formation of the canon as a basis for establishing the priority of church authority, the *testimonium ecclesiae.*

In section 2 Calvin responds to the Roman concept of *testimonium ecclesiae* with arguments drawn from the New Testament and from history.

> These ravings are admirably refuted by a single expression of an apostle. Paul testifies that the Church is "built on the foundation of the apostles and prophets" (Eph. 2:20). If the doctrine of the apostles and prophets is the foundation of the Church, the former must have had its certainty before the latter began to exist. . . . For if the Christian Church was founded at first on the writings of the prophets, and the preaching of the apostles, that doctrine, wheresoever it may be found, was certainly ascertained and sanctioned and antecedently to the Church, since, but for this, the Church herself never could have existed.[5]

Thus for Calvin the internal testimony of the Spirit is vital not only to theology in general but to ecclesiology in particular. The church is subordinate to Scripture, not the Scripture to the church.

The relationship of church to canon is critical to the conclusion of section 2. Here Calvin sets forth the classic Reformation view of church and canon:

> Nothing, therefore, can be more absurd than the fiction, that the power of judging Scripture is in the Church, and that on her nod its certainty depends. When the church receives it, and gives it the stamp of her authority, she does not make that authentic which was otherwise doubtful or controverted, but acknowledging it as the truth of God, she, as in duty bound, shows her reverence by an unhesitating assent.[6]

Here Calvin does not vitiate church authority but places it in its proper subordinate perspective. The church is indeed active in the historical process of canon formation. But the crucial point is that the church neither *creates* nor *validates* the canon. The canon has prior authority and validity. What the church does in the historical process of canon development is to receive it, acknowledge it to be the truth of God, show reverence to it, and give *unhestitating assent* to it. Note again the proper action of the church according to Calvin:

> 1) *receive,* 2) *acknowledge,* 3) *revere,* 4) *assent.* These terms indicate that the Church does not create the authority of Scripture but recognizes and assents to an authority which is already there. Characteristically Calvin chooses his words carefully, perhaps with a view to the terminology of the Muratorian Canon which was *recipere.*[7]

The role of the church in "receiving" and "acknowledging" the Scripture is echoed in the Reformed confessions, which follow Calvin at this point.[8]

In section 3 Calvin responds to the Roman appeal to Augustine's famous statement in which he says that he would not believe the gospel were he not moved by the authority of the church. First Calvin locates the context of Augustine's remarks—the Manichaean controversy—and goes on to say:

> Augustine, therefore, does not here say that the faith of the godly is founded on the authority of the Church; nor does he mean that the certainty of the gospel depends upon it; he merely says that the unbelievers would have no certainty

95

of the gospel, so as thereby to win Christ, were they not influenced by the consent of the Church. And he clearly shows this to be his meaning, by thus expressing himself a little before: "When I have praised my own creed, and ridiculed yours, who do you suppose is to judge between us; or what more is to be done than to quit those who, inviting us to certainty, afterward command us to believe uncertainty, and follow those who invite us, in the first instance, to believe what we are not yet able to comprehend, that waxing stronger through faith itself, we may become able to understand what we believe—no longer men, but God Himself internally strengthening and illuminating our minds."[9]

This last citation from Augustine captures the essence of Calvin's understanding of Augustine. From that quotation we see an incipient expression of Augustine's own doctrine of the *testimonium*. Calvin concludes that the obvious inference to be drawn from Augustine is

that this holy man had no intention to suspend our faith in Scripture on the nod of decision of the Church, but only to intimate (what we too admit to be true) that those who are not yet enlightened by the Spirit of God, become teachable by reverence for the Church, and thus submit to learn the faith of Christ from the gospel. . . . But he nowhere insinuates that the authority which we give to the Scriptures depends on the definitions or devices of men. He only brings forward the universal judgment of the Church, as a point most pertinent to the cause, and one, moreover, in which he had the advantage of his opponents.[10]

96

In section 4 Calvin presents his view of the relationship between the *testimonium* and other evidence for the authority of Scripture. Calvin begins by asserting the superiority of the "secret testimony of the Spirit" to human conjecture. He says:

> Hence, the biggest proof of Scripture is uniformly taken from the character whose word it is. . . . Our conviction of the truth of Scripture must be derived from a higher source than human conjectures, judgments, or reasons; namely, the secret testimony of the Spirit.[11]

Here Calvin makes it clear that the *testimonium* serves as the ultimate and highest ground of certainty for the believer. The *testimonium* is not placed over against reason as a form of mysticism or subjectivism. Rather, it goes beyond and transcends reason. Calvin says:

> But I answer, that the testimony of the Spirit is superior to reason. For as God alone can properly bear witness to his own words, so these words will not obtain full credit on the hearts of men, until they are sealed by the inward testimony of the Spirit.[12]

Calvin's statement that "the testimony of the Spirit is superior to reason" may lead some to conclude that the reformer indulges in a flight into irrationality as a final defense for the authority of Scripture. D. F. Strauss, for example, in the nineteenth century, called this article the "Achilles Heel of Protestantism," because it moved authority out of the objectivity of revelation into the subjectivity of a secret experience that is confined to the hidden chambers of the human heart.[13]

From what follows (namely an entire chapter devoted to objective evidence for biblical authority) it is clear that Calvin is not guilty of such subjectivistic fancy. For Calvin the *testimonium* is not irrational but transrational. That is, it does not move against reason but beyond it. If this is in any way ambiguous in section 4, it becomes manifestly clear in section 5.

The introduction to section 5 gives the clearest statement of the relationship of the *testimonium* to objective evidence we can find in the *Institutes*. Calvin writes:

> Let it therefore be held as fixed, that those who are inwardly taught by the Holy Spirit acquiesce implicitly in Scripture; that Scripture, carrying its own evidence along with it, deigns not to submit to proofs and arguments, but owes the full conviction with which we ought to receive it to the testimony of the Spirit.[14]

The crucial phrases in this summary statement are (1) "acquiesce implicitly in Scripture" and (2) "Scripture, carrying its own evidence along with it." These two phrases highlight the balance of subjectivity and objectivity in Calvin's *testimonium*. The effect of the internal testimony is that the believer *acquiesces* to Scripture. The internal testimony offers no new argument or content to the evidence found in Scripture objectively, but so works in our hearts that we are willing to submit to what is already there.

The concept of *acquiesence* is critical to our understanding of Calvin and thus worthy of further consideration.

Calvin here uses the Latin verb *acquiesce*, which corresponds to the English meaning: "to rest satisfied or apparently satisfied, or to rest without opposition and discontent: usually implying previous opposition, uneasiness or dislike, but ultimate compliance or submission; as to *acquiesce* in the dispensations of Providence. Syn.—accede, agree, consent, submit, yield, comply, concur, conform."[15] The implicit connotation of this *acquiescence* is agreement "without reservation or doubt."[16] We see it earlier in Augustine's development of the concept of the *fides implicitum*.[17]

Thus Calvin describes the effect of the *testimonium* in terms of the believer's unqualified assent to or yielding to the Scripture. Where the believer formerly was "tossed to and fro in a sea of doubts," he now rests peaceably in the assurance that the Bible is indeed the Word of God.

The second crucial phrase, "that Scripture, carrying its own evidence along with it, deigns not to submit . . . " calls attention to the fact that, for Calvin, the *testimonium* does not function in a vacuum. There is an inseparable relationship between *testimonium* and *objective evidence*. The *testimonium* does not function either against the evidence or apart from the evidence but produces *acquiescence* to the evidence. The Scripture objectively gives evidence that it is the Word of God. The Spirit does not prove true what gives evidence of being false but rather gives us the quiet assurance that the evidence is certain. The Spirit causes us to submit or yield to the evidence. Our yielding is a subjective act to an objective basis of evidence.

If the relationship between *testimonium* and evidence is in any way vague in chapter 7, it becomes clear in chapter 8, in which Calvin enumerates the *indicia* or evidence the

Scriptures have for their divine origin and authority. He speaks of the dignity of the matter, the heavenliness of its doctrine, the content of its parts, the majesty of its style, the antiquity of its teaching, the sincerity of its narrative, its miracles, predictive prophecies fulfilled, its use through the ages, and its witness by the blood of the martyrs. He sees this evidence not as being weak and tentative but objectively strong and compelling. He says of the Scriptures' own evidence:

> True, were I called to contend with the craftiest despisers of God, I trust, though I am not possessed of the highest ability or eloquence, I should not find it difficult to stop their obstreperous mouths; I could, without much ado, put down the boastings which they mutter in corners, were anything to be gained by refuting their cavils.[18]

Again Calvin writes:

> There are other reasons, neither few nor feeble, by which the dignity and majesty of the Scriptures may not be only proved to the pious, but also completely vindicated against the cavils of slanderers.[19]

The *indicia* provide objective evidence that Calvin calls "proof." To refuse to submit to this evidence is regarded as caviling and a form of slander. Those who contend against Scripture are called obstreperous. However, in spite of the number and the power of the *indicia*, they remain incapable, in themselves, of producing a "firm faith" in

Scripture unless they are accompanied by the *testimonium*. Calvin says:

> These [*indicia*], however, cannot of themselves produce a firm faith in Scripture until our heavenly Father manifest his presence in it, and thereby secure implicit reverence for it. . . . Still the human testimonies which go to confirm it will not be without effect, if they are used in subordination to that chief and highest proof as secondary helps to our weakness. But it is foolish to attempt to prove to infidels that the Scripture is the Word of God. This cannot be known to be, except by faith.[20]

The question Calvin leaves for us is, Why, if the *indicia* are so strong objectively, do they fail to yield certainty? Why, that is, is the *testimonium* necessary?

To answer this question we must look to Calvin's view of the depravity of man and consequently to the noetic effects of sin. We must say that man's problem with certainty here is not so much an intellectual problem as a moral, or spiritual, one. To be sure, the moral problem touches heavily on the intellect, since the prejudice of the heart against God clouds the mind and makes it "dark."

The Problem of Certainty

Since the *testimonium* is related to our certainty concerning the authority of Scripture, it is important for us to have a clear understanding of what we mean by *certainty*. The word provokes much discussion and not a little confusion, inasmuch as it is capable of different technical and common usages. Let me enumerate three distinct ways in which the word *certainty* may be used.

Philosophical or Formal Certainty

Philosophical certainty has to do with formal arguments that are so logically tight and compelling that to deny the conclusion would be to yield to manifest irrationality or absurdity. This kind of certainty can be found only within the framework of the formal relationship of propositions. The components of a syllogism serve to illustrate this. Let us examine the classical model syllogism to illustrate formal certainty:

Premise A: All men are mortal.
Premise B: Socrates is a man.
Conclusion: Socrates is mortal.

In this syllogism the canons of logic dictate that *if* premise A is true *and* premise B is true, then the conclusion is necessarily, by resistless logic, true. Note, however, that the truth of the conclusion, though it flows irresistibly from the premises, is still ultimately dependent on the truth of the premises. Unless we can demonstrate the truth of the premises we cannot claim absolute certainty for the conclusion. Thus the certainty of the conclusion is conditioned by and dependent on the certainty of the premises. Though the conclusion follows necessarily from the premises, it could conceivably be false if one or both of the premises is false. To state it another way, the conclusion could be formally valid but still not be materially true.

With the syllogism in view, do we know with absolute certainty that Socrates was in fact mortal? Since the conclusion rests on its premises, let us examine the certainty quotient of the premises.

Do we know with certainty that all men are mortal? If so, how do we know it? By reason? By sense perception? Could we possibly prove this statement to be true? To prove it absolutely we would have to examine every human being who has ever lived and is now alive to prove our claim. Here we run head-on into the limits of induction. To know inductively that all men are mortal we would have to observe the death of all men, including ourselves! The only way we could have absolute certainty that all men are mortal would be posthumously! It may seem ridiculous to say we do not know all men are mortal in light of the overwhelming evidence to the fact that human beings die. Millions of mortal humans have come and gone and precious few have escaped death. Even Christ died. (The notable exceptions include Enoch and Elijah. Even these two, though spared death, were never said to be *incapable* of dying.) But we are speaking here of strict, absolute certainty. Until all the data is in, we cannot make absolute universal assertions on the basis of induction. Thus an element of uncertainty, however minuscule, attends the assertion of premise A.

What about premise B? How do we know that Socrates was a man? Maybe he was an angel in disguise. Perhaps he was bionic or a figment of the creative imagination of Plato. We trust the reports of fallible men of antiquity for our information about Socrates. We have a high degree of probability that there really was a Socrates but we lack absolute certainty.

Absolute philosophical certainty is limited to relative and conditional formal relationships of propositions. We can never achieve such certainty about the real world as long as we are dependent in any way on induction. This should not lead us to undue skepticism about the possibility of knowledge but simply to a healthy awareness of the limits of our faculties of knowledge. These limits are a part of our creatureliness. As long as our capacity for knowledge is the slightest bit less than omniscient, then the problem of philosophical certainty will remain. Only a being who is omniscient can transcend the problem. In other words, only God can have philosophical certainty. Since we are not and cannot be gods, we are left with philosophical uncertainty.

Confidence as Certainty

In spite of the above consideration, we still answer many questions in our lives routinely by using the word *certainly.* We make assertions to which some respond, "Are you sure?" We reply, "Yes." But how can we be *sure* about anything if absolute certainty is beyond the scope of our ability?

Obviously when we speak of being "sure" of things or say "certainly," we are speaking about a kind of certainty that is not the same as a technical philosophical certainty. Here we are using the word *certain* in a way that describes a particular feeling state that attends a given idea or assertion. Here the word *certain* describes a sense of confidence or assurance. Such a certainty can manifest relative degrees of intensity, since it is more or less subjected to a mixture of doubt.

Moral Certainty

The third variety of certainty may be termed *moral certainty* or *juridical* certainty. This is the certainty of the law courts when they use the expression "beyond reasonable doubt." Suppose we have a case of a person who committed cold-blooded murder in the presence of five hundred witnesses and whose ruthless act was captured by a broadcast television camera. To compound the evidence, the culprit was arrested while holding a smoking gun, which fired the fatal bullet and which clearly bears his fingerprints. The cumulative weight of this evidence is presented by the prosecution at the trial of the accused.

Suppose now that the defense attorney for the accused seeks exoneration on the basis of an appeal to the lack of absolute certainty concerning the guilt of his client. He argues that (1) the five hundred witnesses suffered a mass hallucination; (2) the television account was a carefully contrived electronic charade; (3) the ballistics report matching the fatal bullet with the firearm found in the hands of his client suffers the lack of the certainty found in all inductive studies involving empirical evidence; (4) the fact that his client's fingerprints match the prints taken from the gun is admitted by the lawyer, but he argues that this represents the first occasion in history where two different people are found to have identical sets of fingerprints. Thus the defense rests its case on a philosophical appeal to the theoretical possibility that his client is a victim of strange and extraordinary circumstances. The circumstantial evidence amassed by the prosecution is presented as being less than absolutely certain so the defense asks for acquittal on the basis of "reasonable doubt."

How do we respond to such a bizarre scenario? The doubt raised by the defense may indeed be *rational*, but is it *reasonable?* The courts recognize the difference. Without a distinction between formal certainty and moral or juridical certainty, it would be impossible to convict anyone of a crime unless God himself were both prosecutor and judge.

Thus moral certainty refers to certainty acquired from the weight of evidence that, though lacking in philosophical certainty, is weighty enough to impose moral culpability. It is precisely this kind of certainty that the *indicia* of Scripture yield.

Though Calvin does not articulate the kind of distinction outlined above, it is spelled out by his disciples. Benjamin Breckinridge Warfield, for example, cites Johannes Andreas Quenstedt on this point:

> The exact relations of the "proofs" to the divinity of Scripture, which Calvin teaches, was sufficiently clear to be caught by his successors. It is admirably stated in the Westminster Confession of Faith. And we may add that the same conception is stated also very precisely by Quenstedt: "These motives, as well internal as external, by which we are led to the knowledge of the authority of Scripture, make the theopneusty of Sacred Scripture *probable,* and produce a *certitude which is not merely conjectural but moral* . . . they do not make the divinity of Scripture infallible and altogether indubitable. . . . That is to say, they are not of the nature of *demonstration,* but nevertheless give *moral certitude.* "[21]

The bridge from moral certitude to full assurance is constructed uniquely by the *testimonium.* The testimony of the

Spirit puts the heart at rest and at peace regarding the authority of Scripture.

Heart or Head as the Object of the *Testimonium?*

Is the *testimonium* a cognitive act of the Spirit, involving primarily the human intellect, or is the primacy of the Spirit's activity located in the heart or the will? If we examine the *Institutes* we see that in sections 4 and 5 of chapter 7 Calvin alternates between mind and heart. He refers to the heart four times and to the mind three times. This makes for some difficulty in locating the primacy of Calvin's thrust.

Perhaps the solution to this difficulty may be found in the Reformer's qualifications of the kind of faith that is affected by the *testimonium*. Calvin speaks of "full faith" (1.7.4), "full credit in the hearts of men" (1.7.4), "full conviction" (1.7.5), "feel perfectly assured" (1.7.5), "true faith" (1.7.5), "full conviction" (1.8.1), and "firm faith" (1.8.13).

Only the Spirit can produce the fullness of faith and conviction Calvin speaks of. The *indicia* alone do not have the power to produce that kind of faith. Warfield says of this dimension:

This prevalent misapprehension of Calvin's meaning is due to neglect to observe the precise thing for which he affirms the *indicia* to be ineffective and the precise reason he assigns for this ineffectiveness. There is only one thing which he says they cannot do: that is to produce "sound faith." . . . And their failure to produce "sound faith" is due solely to the *subjective condition* of man, which is such that a creative operation of the Holy Spirit in the soul is requisite before he can exercise "sound faith."[22]

It is thus the sinful condition of fallen man that makes the *testimonium* necessary. Inasmuch as, outside of grace, the heart is indisposed toward God, the mind refuses to embrace the Scripture. Here we see a parallel with the Reformation tripartite notion of faith as being composed of *notia*, *assensus*, and *fiducia*. The *indicia* is sufficient to produce *assensus* but not *fiducia*. Herein we may discern what Calvin means by *full* faith. It is a faith that goes beyond mere intellectual assent to an acquiescence of the heart and will to the Word of God.

Again Warfield notes: "The testimony of the Spirit is the subjective preparation of the heart to receive the objective evidence in a sympathetic embrace."[23] Again, quoting Theodore Beza, Warfield writes:

> The testimony of the Spirit of adoption does not lie properly in this, that we believe to be true what the Scriptures testify (for this is known also to the devils and many of the lost), but rather in this—that each applies to himself the promise of salvation in Christ of which Paul speaks in Romans 8:15–16.[24]

The Lutheran David Hollaz echoes the thought of Beza on this point:

> The testimony of the Holy Spirit is the supernatural act (*actus supernaturalis*) of the Holy Spirit by means of the Word of God alternatively read or heard . . . by which the heart of man is moved, opened, illuminated, turned to the obedi-

ence of faith, so that the illuminated man out of these internal spiritual movements truly perceives the Word which is propounded to him to have proceeded from God, and gives it therefore his unwavering assent.[25]

Thus the *testimonium* is directed primarily at the heart of man, with the effect on the mind being a consequence of the change of the disposition of the heart. The *testimonium* is not a secret new argument or separate cognitive revelation that supplements the *indicia*. No new content is transmitted to the believer's mind by the *testimonium*. The *testimonium*, as Warfield points out, "is not a propositional revelation, but an instinctive 'sense.' "[26]

Neoorthodox Views of the *Testimonium*

With the advent of dialectical, crisis, or neoorthodox views of Scripture, a noticeable shift occurred in thinking concerning the *testimonium*. In reaction against a formal, objectivized view of Scripture, neoorthodoxy offered a more kinetic or dynamic view of Scripture and revelation.

Over against a schema that views the Bible as the Word of God in *esse*, the neoorthodox school located the objectivity of the Word of God uniquely in the person of Christ. He alone embodies or incarnates the Word. Revelation occurs as the Spirit speaks to us through the *instrument* of Scripture. Scripture is not itself revelation but is a *vehicle* of or witness (*zeugnis*) to revelation. It becomes revelatory as the Spirit speaks through it. The Scripture, then, is a vehicle of the divine-human encounter. Without the activity of the Spirit the Scripture cannot be viewed as objective revelation.

For Calvin the *testimonium* results in a subjective acquiescence to an objective revelation. The Bible is the Word of God with or without the internal testimony. For neoorthodoxy, the Bible is not the Word of God *in essence* but only a vehicle of revelation. It may or may not be the Word of God, depending on the testimony of the Spirit. Objectivity is restricted to Christ and does not extend to the biblical writings.

Following the lead of Martin Kähler,[27] Emil Brunner writes:

> I believe, however, in contrast to the Apostle, in Jesus Christ *by means of* that which He proclaims to me by the Apostle, who bears witness to Christ. The witness of the Apostle is an *instrument* of the divine revelation to me. But I do not give credence to the witness of the Apostle because the Apostle is represented to me as a trustworthy witness, and because I have already been assured that he is "inspired"; but I believe his witness at the same moment that I believe in the Christ to whom he testifies since his witness becomes to me the Word of God through the fact that God, through His Spirit, permits it to dawn on me as the Word of His truth. . . . In one act of revelation there is created within me faith in Christ, and faith in the Scriptures which testify of Him. . . . The Scriptures are indeed the first of the means which God uses, but they are not the first *object* of faith, nor are they the *ground* of my faith. The ground, the authority, which moves me to faith is no other than Jesus Christ Himself, as He speaks to me from the pages of the Scriptures through the Holy Spirit, as my Lord and my Redeemer.

This is what men of old used to call the *testimonium spiritus sancti internum.*[28]

Time out! On the contrary, this is *not* what men of old used to call the *testimonium.* As we have shown above, the function of the *testimonium* is not to provide us with revelatory content but to provide us with certainty and assurance that the Bible is the revelatory Word of God.

We quite agree with Brunner that the Scriptures are not the object of our faith. Brunner is here guarding against any form of bibliolatry, in which faith in the Bible supplants faith in Christ. But it is one thing to say the Bible is not the *object* of our faith and quite another to say the Bible does not contain *objective revelation* of the object of my faith. Brunner and other such interpreters throw out the baby with the bathwater and leave us ensnared in an existential quagmire of subjectivity.

Emphasizing the "event" of revelation in terms of personal encounter,[29] Brunner goes on to describe the dynamics of the revelation experience:

> The revelation in Jesus Christ produces the *illumination* in my heart and mind, so that I can now see: that this man is the Christ. Suddenly, all the barriers of time and space have faded away; I have become "contemporary" with Christ. . . . [30] He is no more external than my faith is external. The sense of spatial and temporal remoteness, all external objectivity, has disappeared: He who previously spoke to me only from the outside now speaks within me through the Holy Spirit. . . . The knowledge of the Scriptures as the Word of God is the same as the experience of the Holy Spirit. The truth is neither subjective nor objec-

tive, but it is both at once; it is the truth which may be described in other words, as the encounter of the human "I" with God's "thou" in Jesus Christ.[31]

Shades of Sören Kierkegaard and truth as subjectivity. Brunner says that truth is not subjective. This would seem to relieve him of the charge of *subjectivism*. But then he maintains that the truth is not *objective* either. This would seem to warrant the charge. Then he says it is *both* at once. How do we understand this?

Perhaps all that Brunner means is that truth contains both objective and subjective elements. Maybe what we have here is a restatement of Calvin that the Bible is objectively the Word of God, to which the Spirit moves us to make a subjective, personal response. All truth is "personal" in the sense that for it to have subjective meaning for me I must have some kind of personal response to it, either positively or negatively. But Brunner has already made it clear that this is not what he means. Truth as such is not objective but dynamic and personal. This is a kind of *personalism* that redefines the nature of truth. Here truth is not truth until or unless the personal dimension is added. Here we see the crisis of *propositional* revelation that was triggered by the neoorthodox movement.

No one would argue that biblical truth demands personal response; that is axiomatic. The issue is, Do we have an objective revelatory truth to respond to?

Thomas F. Torrance develops the concept of the role of the Spirit in relationship to the Word in his essay "The Epistemological Relevance of the Holy Spirit." He initiates this study by saying, "The epistemological relevance of the Holy

Spirit lies in the dynamic and transformal aspects of this knowledge."[32]

Following a phenomenological pattern of thought similar to Brunner's, in which the accent is on the kinetic experimental character of revelation, Torrance says:

> On the one hand, then, the Holy Spirit through His presence brings the very Being of God to bear upon us in our experience, creating the relation to the divine Being which knowledge of God requires in order to be knowledge, but on the other hand the Spirit through His ineffable and self-effacing nature reinforces the impossibility of our conceiving in thought and expressing in speech how our thought and speech are related to God, so that our thoughts and statements by referring infinitely beyond themselves break off before Him in wonder, adoration and silence, that God may be in All in all. Through the Spirit empirical relation to the divine Being takes place and within it we are given intuitive knowledge of God, but the mode of our relation to Him and the mode of our knowledge of Him must be in accordance with His nature as *Spirit*, and therefore even though we have empirical relation to Him and intuitive knowledge of Him, they are not amenable to the kind of control which we exercise in relation to creaturely objects. It is rather we who fall under the overwhelming presence of the divine Being and come under the control of His spirit in our experience and knowledge of Him.[33]

With Torrance the accent is on kinetic, transformal, experimental, intuitive knowledge of God via the Spirit and the Word. With this accent it is not surprising to see Torrance liken his approach to that of Martin Heidegger. He says, "We may want to compare it to Heidegger's leap of thought to open up the original source of being."[34]

Thus to escape formalism or objectivism the Spirit becomes the springboard to transpropositional knowledge of God. From this shift in understanding of Calvin's *testimonium* we readily see how the next critical problem of theology became the God-talk controversy that culminated in the death-of-God movement. If the content of revelation (not merely the internal assurance of its veracity) becomes separated from objectivity, there is no avoiding the crisis of linguistic analysis. The "dynamic" of "kinetic thinking" leaves us only with intuition. But what about cognitive knowledge of God?

It is the internal dimension of the *testimonium* that makes it vulnerable to a subjectivistic bent. If the *testimonium* has reference to the revelation itself, rather than to an inner assurance that corroborates external objective evidence (*indicia*), there remains no authority above and beyond the private experience of the believing individual. If the Word becomes subject to the internal dynamics of the believing individual, it becomes no longer the objective Word of God but the subjective word of man. This is a grave crisis inherent in an existential approach to revelation.

For Calvin the believing individual makes a subjective response to the objective Word through the impetus of the Spirit. For the existentialist, the subjective response determines the Word as it becomes the Word of God only through the kinetic activity of the Spirit.

Though orthodoxy faces a modern intramural debate regarding the apologetic value and function of the *testimo-*

nium, there is a monolithic consensus among those divided over apologetics for the objective, propositional character of the Bible as the Word of God.

The New Testament Basis for the *Testimonium*

The New Testament does not provide us with a thoroughgoing exposition of the "internal testimony" as such. This, at face value, could expose John Calvin, Martin Luther, and a host of other theologians to the charge that the doctrine has been constructed on the basis of speculative philosophy or by a "system" of theology imposed on the Scriptures arbitrarily. However, the New Testament is replete with allusions to the work of the Spirit in securing our confidence in the Word.[35] These references are scattered throughout the New Testament and include such classic texts as 2 Corinthians 4:3–6; 1 John 1:10; 2:14; 5:20; Colossians 2:2; 1 Thessalonians 1:5; Galatians 4:6; Romans 8:15–16; and others.

The work of revelation, illumination, and persuasion are carried on from a trinitarian framework, ranging from the Father's revealing Jesus' messianic identity to Peter at Caesarea Phillipi (Matt. 16:17), to Jesus' revelation of the things taught him by the Father in secret (John 12:49–50), to the work of the Spirit in illumination. Though all members of the Trinity are active in this redemptive operation, it is the work of the Holy Spirit that is stressed by the New Testament.

Consider 1 Corinthians 2:4–11 as a classic text for the *testimonium:*

. . . And my speech and my preaching were not with persuasive words of human wisdom, but in demonstration of the Spirit and of power, that your faith should not be in the wisdom of men but in the power of God.

However, we speak wisdom among those who are mature, yet not the wisdom of this age, nor of the rulers of this age, who are coming to nothing. But we speak the wisdom of God in a mystery, the hidden wisdom which God ordained before the ages for our glory, which none of the rulers of this age knew; for had they known, they would not have crucified the Lord of glory.

But as it is written:

"Eye has not seen,
   nor ear heard,
Nor have entered into the heart of man
The things which God has prepared
   for those who love him."

But God has revealed them to us through His Spirit. For the Spirit searches all things, yes, the deep things of God. For what man knows the things of a man except the spirit of the man which is in him? Even so no one knows the things of God except the Spirit of God.

The theme of this passage is the supremacy of the power of God in revelation. The Spirit searches things that go beyond what the senses perceive. Our faith is said to "stand" in the power of God. God reveals the secret things of himself *through* the *Spirit*. The Holy Spirit mediates the Word. As the Apostle Paul notes later: "These things we also speak, not in words which man's wisdom teaches but which the

Holy Spirit teaches, comparing spiritual things with spiritual" (1 Cor. 2:13). Here Paul links the apostolic words with the work of the Spirit. The Spirit is not mentioned merely as being the *source* of the content but as being the basis of the *persuasive power* of the words.

The same emphasis on revelation and persuasion may be seen in 2 Corinthians 3:1–11. The writing of the Spirit on the Christian's heart is not viewed as a gnostic, esoteric experience, but as a powerful penetration of the heart by the truth of the content of God's revelation.[36]

The internal testimony is not an isolated work of the Spirit ripped loose from the written Word. Rather, as the Trinity works in harmony to effect our redemption, so the Spirit bears witness and testifies to us inwardly of the whole content of divine revelation.

PART 2

THE INERRANCY

SCRIPTURE

5

THE WORD OF GOD
AND AUTHORITY

he Chicago Statement on Biblical Inerrancy, adopted at a meeting of more than two hundred evangelical leaders in October 1978, rightly affirms that "the authority of Scripture is a key issue for the Christian church in this and every age." But authority cannot stand in isolation, as the Statement shows. The authority of the Bible is based on its being the written Word of God, and because the Bible is the Word of God and the God of the Bible is truth and speaks truthfully, authority is linked to inerrancy. If the Bible is the Word of God, and if God is a God of truth, then the Bible must be inerrant—not merely in some of its parts, as some modern theologians are saying, but totally, as the church for the most part has said down through the ages of its history.

Some of the terms used in the debate about the authority and inerrancy of the Bible are technical ones. Some show

121

up in the Chicago Statement, but they are not difficult to come to understand. They can be mastered (and the doctrine of inerrancy more fully understood) by a little reading and study. This commentary on the Chicago Statement attempts to provide such material in reference to the Nineteen Articles of Affirmation and Denial, which form the heart of the document. The full text of the statement appears as appendix 2.

ARTICLE I: Authority

We affirm that the Holy Scriptures are to be received as the authoritative World of God. We deny that the Scriptures receive their authority from the church, tradition, or any other human source.

The initial article of the Chicago Statement is designed to establish the degree of authority that is to be attributed to the Bible. This article, as well as article II, makes the statement clearly a Protestant one. Though it is true that the Roman Catholic Church has consistently and historically maintained a high view of the inspiration of Holy Scripture, there remains the unresolved problem of the uniqueness and sufficiency of biblical authority for the church.

Rome has placed alongside of Scripture the traditions of the church as a supplement to Scripture and, consequently, a second source of special revelation beyond the scope of Scripture.

It has been a continuous assertion of the Roman Catholic Church that since the church established the extent and scope of the New Testament and Old Testament canon, there is a certain sense in which the authority of the Bible is subordinate to and dependent upon the church's approval. It is particularly these issues of the relationship of church and canon and of the question of multiple sources of special revelation that are in view with both article I and article II.

In earlier drafts of article I, the extent of this canon was spelled out to include the 66 canonical books that are found and embraced within the context of most Protestant-sanctioned editions of the Bible. In discussions among the participants of the Summit and because of requests to the drafting committee, there was considerable sentiment for striking the words "66 canonical books" from the earlier drafts. This was due to some variance within Christendom as to the exact number of books that are to be recognized within the canon. For example, the Ethiopic Church has more books included in their canon than 66. The final draft affirms simply that the *Holy Scriptures* are to be received as the authoritative Word of God. For the vast majority of Protestants the designation "Holy Scripture" has clear reference to the 66 canonical books, but it leaves room for those who differ on the canon question to participate in the confession of the nature of Scripture. The specific question of the number of books contained in that canon is left open in this Statement.

The whole question of the scope of canon, or the list of books that make up our Bible, may be one that confuses many people, particularly those who are accustomed to a clearly defined number of books by their particular church confessions. Some have argued that if one questions a particular book's canonicity, this carries with it the implication that one does not believe in a divinely inspired Bible. Perhaps the clearest illustration of this in history is the fact that Martin Luther, at one point in his ministry, had strong reservations about including the book of James in the New Testament canon. Though it is abundantly clear that Luther believed in an inspired Bible, he still had questions about whether or not a particular book should be included in that inspired Bible. Several scholars have tried to deny that Luther ever believed in inspiration because of his questioning of the book of James. Here it is very important to see the difference between the question of the scope of the canon and the question of the inspiration of the books which are recognized as included in the canon. In other words, the nature of Scripture and the question of the extent of Scripture are two different questions which must not be confused.

A key word in the affirmation section of article I is the word *received*. The initial draft mentioned that the Scriptures are to be received by the church. The phrase "by the church" has been deleted because it is clear that the Word of God in Holy Scripture is to be received not only by the church but by everyone. The word *received* has historical significance. In the church councils that considered the canon question, the Latin word *recipimus* was used, meaning "we receive" the following books to be included in the canon. In that usage of the word *receive*, it is clear that the church was not declaring certain books to be authoritative by virtue of the church's prior authority, but that the church was simply acknowledging the Word of God to be the Word of God. By the word *receive* they displayed their willingness to submit to what they regarded to be already the Word of God. Consequently, any notion that the church creates the Bible or is superior to the Bible is eliminated.

If any ambiguity about the relationship of Scripture to the church remains in the affirmation, it is removed in the subsequent denial: The Scriptures receive their authority from God, not from the church nor from any other human source.

ARTICLE II: Scripture and Tradition

We affirm that the Scriptures are the supreme written norm by which God binds the conscience, and that the authority of the church is subordinate to that of Scripture. We deny that church creeds, councils, or declarations have authority greater than or equal to the authority of the Bible.

Article II of the Chicago Statement reinforces article I and goes into more detail concerning the matters involved with it. Article II has in view the classical Protestant principle of *sola Scriptura,* which speaks of the unique authority of the Bible with respect to binding the consciences of men. The affirmation of article II speaks of the Scriptures as "the supreme written norm." Discussion concerning the word *supreme* was lengthy; alternate words were suggested and subsequently eliminated from the text. Words like *ultimate* and *only* were discarded in favor of *supreme.* The question at this point dealt with the fact that other written documents are important to the life of the church. For example, church creeds and confessions form the basis of subscription and unity of faith in many different Christian denominations and communities. Such creeds and confessions have a kind of normative authority within a given Christian body and have the effect of binding consciences within that particular context. However, it is a classic tenet of Protestants to recognize that all such creeds and confessions are fallible and cannot fully and finally bind the conscience of an individual believer. Only the Word of God has the kind of authority that can bind

125

the conscience of men forever. So, though the articles acknowledge that there are other written norms recognized by different bodies of Christians, insofar as they are true, those written norms are derived from and are subordinate to the supreme written norm which is the Holy Scripture.

In the denial it is clearly spelled out that no church creed, council, or declaration has authority greater than or equal to the authority of the Bible. Again, any idea of an equal authority level of tradition or church officers is repudiated by this statement. The whole question of a Christian's obedience to authority structures apart from the Scripture was a matter of great discussion with regard to this article. For example, the Bible itself exhorts us to obey the civil magistrates. We are certainly willing to subject ourselves to our own church confessions and to the authority structure of our ecclesiastical bodies. But the thrust of this article is to indicate that whatever lesser authorities there are, they never carry with them the authority of God himself. There is a sense in which all authority in this world is derived and dependent upon the authority of God. God and God alone has intrinsic authority. That intrinsic authority is the authority given to the Bible since it is God's Word. Various Christian bodies have defined the extent of civil authority and ecclesiastical authority in different ways. For example, in Reformed churches the authority of the church is viewed as ministerial and declarative rather than ultimate and intrinsic. God and God alone has the absolute right to bind the consciences of men. Our consciences are justly bound to lesser authorities only when and if they are in conformity to the Word of God.

6

THE WORD OF GOD AND REVELATION

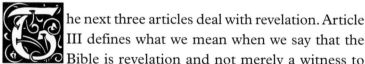he next three articles deal with revelation. Article III defines what we mean when we say that the Bible is revelation and not merely a witness to revelation, as is affirmed by the neoorthodox theologians. Article IV considers the use of human language as a vehicle for divine revelation. Article V notes the way in which the revelation of God unfolds progressively throughout Scripture so that later texts more fully expound the earlier ones. In these articles the framers of the Statement guard against any view which would lessen the unique nature of the Bible as God's written revelation or negate the teaching of some parts of it by appeal to other parts.

ARTICLE III: Revelation

*We **affirm** that the written Word in its entirety is revelation given by God. **We deny** that the Bible is merely a witness to rev-*

elation, or only becomes revelation in encounter, or depends on the responses of men for its validity.

Both the affirmation and denial of article III have in view the controversial question of the objective character of divine revelation in Scripture. There has been considerable debate in the twentieth century on this issue, particularly with the rise of so-called dialectical or "neoorthodox" theology. This approach sought to promote a "dynamic" view of Scripture which sees the authority of Scripture functioning in a dynamic relationship of Word and hearing of the Word. Several theologians have denied that the Bible in and of itself, objectively, is revelation. They maintain that revelation does not occur until or unless there is an inward, subjective human response to that Word. Scholars like Emil Brunner, for example, have insisted that the Bible is not itself revelation, but is merely a witness to that revelation which is found in Christ. It has been fashionable in certain quarters to maintain that special revelation is embodied in Christ and in Christ alone, and that to consider the Bible as objective revelation would be to detract from the uniqueness of the person of Jesus Christ, who is the Word made flesh.

The spirit of these articles is to oppose a disjunction between the revelation that is given to us in the person of Christ objectively and the revelation that comes to us in equally objective terms in the Word of God inscripturated. Here the Bible is seen not merely as a catalyst for revelation but as revelation itself. If the Bible is God's Word, and its content proceeds from him, then its content is to be seen as revelation. Here revelation is viewed as "propositional." It is propositional not because the Bible is written in the style of logical equations or analytical formulas. It is propositional because it communicates a content which may be understood as propositions.

In affirmation of article III the words "in its entirety" are also significant. There are those who have claimed that the Bible contains here and there, in specified places, revelation from God, but that it is the task of the believer individually or the church corporately to separate the parts of Scripture which are revelatory from those which are not. This article by implication repudiates such an approach to Scripture inasmuch as the whole of Scripture, its entire contents, is to be seen as being divine revelation.

The denial stated in article III reinforces the objectivity of revelation in Scripture and maintains that the validity of that revelation does not depend upon human responses. The Bible's truth does not depend in any way on whether or not a person believes the truth.

The central thrust of article III is to declare with confidence that the content of Scripture is not the result of human imagination or cleverly devised philosophical opinions, but that it reflects God's sovereign disclosure about himself and all matters which are touched upon by Scripture. The Bible, then, embodies truth that comes to us from beyond the scope of our own abilities. It comes from God himself.

ARTICLE IV: Human Language

*We **affirm** that God who made mankind in His image has used language as a means of revelation. We **deny** that human language is so limited by our creatureliness that it is rendered inadequate as a vehicle for divine revelation. We further deny that* *the corruption of human culture and language through sin has thwarted God's work of inspiration.*

One of the most significant attacks on biblical inerrancy that has come to light in the twentieth century is that based on the limitations of human language. Since the Bible was not written by God himself but by human writers, the question has emerged again and again whether such human involvement by virtue of the limitations built in human creatureliness would, of necessity, render the Bible less than infallible. Since men are not infallible in and of themselves and are prone to error in all that they do, would it not follow logically that anything coming from the pen of man must be errant? To this we reply, erroneousness is not an inevitable concomitant of human nature. Adam, before the Fall, may well have been free from proneness to error, and Christ, though fully human, never erred. Since the Fall it is a common tendency of men to err. We deny, however, that it is necessary for men to err always and everywhere in what they say or write, even apart from inspiration.

However, with the aid of divine inspiration and the superintendence of the Holy Spirit in the giving of sacred Scripture, the writings of the Bible are free from the normal tendencies and propensities of fallen men to distort the truth. Though our language, and especially our language about God, is never comprehensive and exhaustive in its ability to capture eternal truths, nevertheless it is adequate to give us truth without falsehood. For example, if we made a statement that Chicago is a city in the state of Illinois, the truth communicated by that statement would in no way be exhaustive. That is, all that could possibly be understood of the nature and scope of the city of Chicago would not be known by any human being who made such a statement, nor would all the complexities that go into and comprise the state of Illinois be understood totally by the speaker. Certainly if God made the statement "Chicago is a city in the state of Illinois," within his mind there would be total comprehension of all that is involved in Chicago and Illinois. Nevertheless, the fact that God makes the statement "Chicago is a city in the state of Illinois" would not in itself make the statement more or less true than if a human being made the statement. Though we recognize that human language is limited by creatureliness, we do not allow the inference that therefore human language must necessarily be distortive of truth.

If human language were to be judged intrinsically inadequate to convey revelation, there would be no possible means by which God could reveal anything about himself to us in verbal form. Since, however, the Bible teaches that man is created in the image of God and that there is some point of likeness between man and God, communication between God and man is possible. Such possibility of communication is built into creation by God himself.

With respect to the denial that human language is so limited that it is rendered inadequate, particularly in view of the effects of sin on our human culture and language, we must say that though man's fall renders us guilty before the divine judgment and though "all men are liars," it does not follow necessarily that therefore "all men lie all the time." Though all of us lie at one time or another, this does not mean that we lie every time we speak. Again, that tendency toward corruption, distortion, and falsehood is precisely that which we believe to be overcome by the divine inspi-

131

ration and involvement in the preparation of Holy Scripture. Thus, we think that skepticism about biblical integrity based on inferences drawn from the adequacy or inadequacy of human speech is unwarranted.

ARTICLE V: Progressive Revelation

We affirm that God's revelation within the Holy Scriptures was progressive. We deny that later revelation, which may fulfill earlier revelation, ever corrects or contradicts it. We further deny that any normative revelation has been given since the completion of the New Testament writings.

The issues in view in article V are of profound importance to the life of the church and are very complicated at times. What is simply stated in the affirmation is a recognition that within the Bible itself there is a progressive revelation. All that has been revealed of God in the totality of Scripture is not found, for example, in the book of Genesis. Much of the content of God's redemptive activity in Christ is hinted at in part and given in shadowy ways in the earlier portions of the Old Testament. But throughout sacred Scripture the content of divine revelation is expanded, ultimately to the fullness reached in the New Testament. That is what is meant by progressive revelation in this context, that the revelation within Scripture unfolds in an ever-deepening and broadening way.

Having made that recognition, the article of denial makes clear that such progress and expansion of revelation does not deny or contradict what has been given earlier. Though certain precepts which were obligatory to people in the Old Testament period are no longer so in the New Testament, this

132

does not mean that they were discontinued because they were wicked in the past and now God has corrected what he formerly endorsed, but rather that certain practices have become superseded by new practices that are consistent with fulfillment of Old Testament activities. This in no way suggests that the Old Testament is irrelevant to the New Testament believer or that earlier revelation may be dismissed out of hand in light of newer revelation. The Bible is still to be regarded as a holistic book where the Old Testament helps us understand the New Testament and the New Testament sheds significant light on the Old Testament. Although progressive revelation is recognized, this progressiveness is not to be viewed as a license to play loosely with portions of Scripture, setting one dimension of revelation against another within the Bible itself. The Bible's coherency and consistency is not vitiated by progressive revelation within it.

It is also added by way of denial that no normative revelation has been given to the church since the close of the New Testament canon. The denial does not mean that God the Holy Spirit has stopped working, or that the Holy Spirit in no way leads his people today. Part of the difficulty is that theological words are used in different ways within different Christian communities. For example, what one group may call "revelation" another group may define as "illumination." Thus the qualifying word *normative* is important to understanding the last part of the denial. What is meant here is that no revelation has been given since the first century that merits or warrants inclusion in the canon of Holy Scripture. Private leadings or guidance or "revelations," as some may term them, may not be seen as having the force of authority of Holy Scripture.

133

7

THE WORD OF GOD AND INSPIRATION

nspiration is the way in which God gave his Word to us through human authors, but how he did is a matter not fully understood. In this section of the Articles of Affirmation and Denial, the framers of the document explicitly deny understanding the mode of inspiration. But they affirm, as Scripture itself also does (2 Tim. 3:16), that the Bible is the product of divine inspiration and that his work extended through the human writers to each section and even each word of the original documents. The process of inspiration did not make the biblical writers automatons, for their books reveal differences of vocabulary, style, and other matters of variation between one human author and another. But inspiration did overcome any tendency they may have had to error, with the result that the words they wrote were precisely what God, the divine Author, intended us to have.

ARTICLE VI: Verbal Plenary Inspiration

We affirm that the whole of Scripture and all its parts, down to the very words of the original, were given by divine inspiration. We deny that the inspiration of Scripture can rightly be affirmed of the whole without the parts, or of some parts but not the whole.

What is in view in article VI is the doctrine of verbal plenary inspiration. Plenary inspiration means that the whole of Scripture is given by divine inspiration. Because some have maintained that the whole has been given by inspiration but some parts of that whole are not by divine inspiration, we are speaking of the origin of Scripture, which does not begin with the insights of men but comes from God himself.

In the affirmative section of article VI, we read the phrase "down to the very words of the original." The clause "down to the very words" refers to the extent of inspiration, and the words "of the original" indicate that it is the autographs that were inspired. The limiting of inspiration to the autographs is covered more fully later in article X, though it is plain in this article that the verbal inspiration of the Bible refers to the original manuscripts.

The fact that article VI speaks of divine inspiration down to the very words of the original may conjure up in some people's minds a notion of dictation of the words of Scripture by God. The doctrine of verbal plenary inspiration has often been charged with carrying with it the implication of a dictation theory of inspiration. No such theory is spelled out in this article, nor is it implied. In fact, in article VII the framers of the statement deny the dictation theory.

The issue of dictation has raised problems in church history. In the Council of Trent in the sixteenth century, the Roman Catholic Church did use the word *dictante*, meaning "dictating," with respect to the Spirit's work in the giving of the ancient texts. In the Protestant camp, John Calvin spoke of the biblical writers as being *amanuenses* or secretaries. Added to this is the complex fact that there are portions of Scripture which seem to be given by some form of dictation, such as the Ten Commandments given by God to Moses. However, in the modern era, dictation as a method carries with it the canceling out of human literary styles, vocabulary choices, and the like. This article does not mean to imply such a view of inspiration that would negate or vitiate the literary styles of the individual authors of the biblical documents. The sense in which Calvin, for example, spoke of secretaries and even in which Trent spoke of dictating could hardly be construed to conform to modern methods of dictating using sophisticated equipment such as dictaphones and secretarial transcriptions. The historical context in which these words have been used in the past has specific reference to the fact that inspiration shows some analogy to a man issuing a message that is put together by a secretary. The analogy points to the question of origin of the message. In the doctrine of inspiration what is at stake is the origin of the message from God rather than from human initiation.

The mode of inspiration is left as a mystery by these articles (cf. art. VII). Inspiration, as used here, involves a divine superintendence which preserved the writers in their word choices from using words that would falsify or distort the message of Scripture. Thus, on the one hand, the Statement affirms that God's superintendence and inspiration of the Bible applied down to the very words and, on the other hand, denies that he canceled out the exercise of the writers' personalities in the choices of words used to express the truth revealed.

Evangelical Christians have wanted to avoid the notion that biblical writers were passive instruments like pens in the hands of God, yet at the same time, they affirm that the net result of the process of inspiration would be the same. Calvin, for example, says that we should read the Bible *as if* we have heard God audibly speaking its message. That is, it carries the same weight of authority as if God himself were heard to be giving utterance to the words of Scripture.[1] That does not mean that Calvin believed or taught that God did in fact utter the words audibly. We do not know the process by which inspired Scripture was given. But we are saying that inspiration, however God brought it about, results in the net effect that every word of Scripture carries with it the weight of God's authority.

ARTICLE VII: Inspiration

We affirm *that inspiration was the work in which God by His Spirit, through human writers, gave us His Word. The origin of Scripture is divine. The mode of divine inspiration remains largely a mystery to us.* **We deny** *that inspiration can be reduced to human insight, or to heightened states of consciousness of any kind.*

Article VII spells out in more detail what is implied in article VI. Here clear reference is given to the human writers of the text. The human writers become the human instruments by which God's Word comes to us. Classically, the Holy Scriptures have been called the *Verbum Dei*, the Word of God, or even the *vox Dei*, the voice of God. Yet, at the same time, Holy Scripture comes to us as the words of men. In other words, there is an agency of humanity through which God's divine Word is communicated; yet the origin of Scripture is divine.

What the framers of the document have in view here is the primary meaning of the word *theopneustos* in 2 Timothy 3:16, the word translated "inspired by God." The word *theopneustos* means literally "God breathed" and has primary reference to God's breathing out his Word rather than breathing in some kind of effect upon human writers. So *expiration* is a more accurate term than *inspiration* with respect to the origin of Scripture. But we use the term *inspiration* to cover the concept of the whole process by which the Word comes to us. Initially, it comes from the mouth of God (speaking, of course, metaphorically). From its origin in God it is then transmitted through the agency of human writers under divine supervision and superintendence. The next step in the process of communication is the apprehension of the divine message by human beings. It is explicitly stated in this article that the precise mode by which God accomplishes inspiration remains a mystery. The document makes no attempt to define the "how" of divine inspiration or even to suggest that the method is known to us.

The word *inspiration* can be used and has been used in our language to refer to moments of genius-level insight, of intensified states of consciousness, or of heightened acts of human achievement. We speak of inspired poetry, meaning that the author achieved levels of insight and brilliance that are extraordinary. However, in this dimension of "inspiration" no suggestion is at hand that the source of inspiration is divine power. There are human levels of inspiration reflected in heroic acts, brilliant insights, and intensified states of consciousness. But that is not what is meant by the theological use of the term *inspiration*. Here the statement is making clear that by divine inspiration something transcending all human states of inspiration is in view, something in which the power and supervision of God are at work. Thus, the articles are saying that the Bible, though it is a human book insofar as it is written by human writers, has its humanity transcended by virtue of its divine origin and inspiration.

ARTICLE VIII: Human Authors

We affirm that God in His work of inspiration utilized the distinctive personalities and literary styles of the writers whom He had chosen and prepared. **We deny** that God, in causing these writers to use the very words that He chose, overrode their personalities.

Article VIII reiterates that God's work of inspiration does not cancel out the humanity of the human writers he uses to accomplish his purpose. The writers of Scripture were chosen and prepared by God for their sacred task. However, whatever the process of inspiration may have been, it does not include the canceling of the personality of the writers as they wrote. Though the word is not used in the article, what is clearly in view is a denial of any kind of mechanistic or mechanical inspiration. Mechanical inspiration

140

would reduce the human authors to the level of automatons, robotlike machines. An analysis of Scripture makes clear that the distinctive personalities and writing styles vary from one human writer to another. The style, for example, of Luke is obviously different from that of Matthew. The literary structures found in the writing of Daniel differ greatly from those found, for example, in the writings of James. Men of Hebrew origin tended to write in Hebraic styles, and those of the Greek cultural background tended to write in a Greek style. However, through divine inspiration God made it possible for his truth to be communicated in an inspired way making use of the backgrounds, personalities, and literary styles of these various writers. The human writers were not machines and ought not to be conceived of as being without personality. What is overcome or overridden by inspiration is not human personality, style, or literary structure, but human tendencies to distortion, falsehood, and error.

8

THE WORD OF GOD
AND INERRANCY

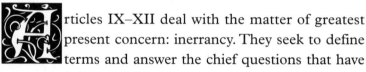rticles IX–XII deal with the matter of greatest present concern: inerrancy. They seek to define terms and answer the chief questions that have been raised: If the Bible has come to us through human authors, which the earlier articles acknowledge, and if it is natural for human beings to err, which all confess, isn't the Bible necessarily errant? Doesn't it cease to be authentically human if it does not have errors? Again, if inerrancy applies properly only to the original manuscripts, called autographs, and if we do not possess these, as we do not, isn't the argument for inerrancy meaningless? Or doesn't it stand only by appealing to documents that do not exist and whose inerrant state cannot be verified? Why can't inerrancy be applied to those parts of the Bible that deal with salvation and not to those parts that deal with history, science, and other "unimportant" and "nonessential" matters?

143

ARTICLE IX: Inerrancy

*We **affirm** that inspiration, though not conferring omniscience, guaranteed true and trustworthy utterance on all matters of which the biblical authors were moved to speak and write. We **deny** that the finitude or fallenness of these writers, by necessity or otherwise, introduced distortion or falsehood into God's Word.*

The affirmation of article IX indicates that inspiration guarantees that the writings of Scripture are true and trustworthy. That is, they are not false, deceptive, or fraudulent in what they communicate.

As we dealt with the problem of the limitations of human language in article IV, so we face now the difficulty of the speaking of truth by creatures who are not omniscient. It is one thing for God to confer infallibility to the writings and quite another to confer omniscience to the writers. Omniscience and infallibility must be carefully distinguished. Although in God they are cojoined, for man it is different. Omniscience refers to the scope of one's knowledge and infallibility to the reliability of his pronouncements. One who knows better can make a false statement if his intentions are to deceive. And, vice versa, a person with limited knowledge can make infallible statements if they can be guaranteed to be completely reliable. Thus we say that though the biblical writings are inspired, this does not imply thereby that the writers knew everything there was to be known or that they were infallible of themselves. The knowledge that they communicate is not comprehensive, but it is true and trustworthy as far as it goes.

The denial of article IX has to do with man's propensity as a finite and fallen creature to introduce distortion or falsehood into God's Word. This was covered from another angle in article IV. But what is in view here is the recurring charge that verbal inspiration or a confession of the inerrancy of Scripture carries with it a docetic view of Scripture. Docetism applies to a particular distortion of the biblical view of Jesus. In the earliest days of the Christian church there were those, usually associated with the school of gnosticism, who believed that Jesus did not really have a human nature or a human body. They argued that he only seemed or appeared to have a human body. This heresy was called docetism from the Greek word *dokeō*, which means to seem, to think, or to appear. Those who denied the reality of the Incarnation and maintained that Jesus had but a phantom body were accused of this heresy. In a more refined and sophisticated sense, docetism has come to apply to any failure to take seriously the real limitations of the human nature of Jesus.

The charge of biblical docetism has been leveled against advocates of inerrancy, most notably by Karl Barth. He accuses us of holding a view of inspiration in which the true humanity of the biblical writers is canceled out by the intrusion of the divine characteristics of infallibility. For Barth it is fundamental to our humanity that we are liable to error. If the classic statement is *errare est humanum*, to err is human, we reply that though it is true that a common characteristic of mankind is to err, it does not follow that men always err or that error is necessary for humanity. If such were to be the case, then it would be necessary for us to assert that Adam, before he fell, had to err or he was not human. And we must also assert that in heaven, in a state of glorification and perfected sanctification, we must con-

THE INERRANCY OF SCRIPTURE

tinue to err if we are to continue to be human. Not only must we ascribe such error to Adam before the Fall and to glorified Christians, we would also have to apply it to the incarnate Christ. Error would be intrinsic to his humanity, and it would have been necessary for Jesus to distort the truth in order to be fully human. Let us never engage in such blasphemy even though we confess the depth to which we have fallen and the high degree of the propensity that we do have to err. Even apart from inspiration, it is not necessary for a human being to err in order to be human. So if it is possible for an uninspired person to speak the truth without error, how much more will it be the case for one who is under the influence of inspiration.

Finitude implies a necessary limitation of knowledge but not necessarily a distortion of knowledge. The trustworthy character of the biblical text should not be denied on the ground of man's finitude.

ARTICLE X: The Autographs

We affirm *that inspiration, strictly speaking, applies only to the autographic text of Scripture, which in the providence of God can be ascertained from available manuscripts with great accuracy. We further affirm that copies and translations of Scripture are the Word of God to the extent that they faithfully represent the original.* *We deny* *that any essential element of the Christian faith is affected by the absence of the autographs. We further deny that this absence renders the assertion of biblical inerrancy invalid or irrelevant.*

Article X deals directly with the perennial issue of the relationship of the text of Scripture that we presently have to the original documents which have not been preserved except through the means of copies. In the first instance, inspiration applies strictly to the original works of the inspired authors. What this does indicate is that the infallible control of God in the production of the original Scripture had not been miraculously perpetuated through the ages in the copying and translating process. It is plainly apparent that there are some minute variations between the manuscript copies that we possess and that the translating process will inject additional variants for those who read the Scripture in another language than Hebrew and Greek. So the framers of the document are not arguing for a perpetually inspired transmission of the text.

Since we do not have the original manuscripts, some have urged that an appeal to the lost originals renders the whole case for the inspiration of the Scripture irrelevant. To reason in this manner is to do despite to the very serious work that has been done in the field of textual criticism. Textual criticism is the science which seeks to reconstruct an original text by a careful analysis and evaluation of the manuscripts we presently possess. This task has to be accomplished with respect to all documents from antiquity that have reached us through manuscript copies. The Old and New Testament Scriptures are probably the texts which have reached us with the most extensive and reliable attestation. For more than ninety-nine percent of the cases, the original text can be reconstructed to a practical certainty. Even in the few cases where some perplexity remains, this does not impinge on the meaning of Scripture to the point of clouding a tenet of the faith or a mandate of life. Thus, in the Bible as we have it (and as it is conveyed to us through faithful translations), we do have for practical purposes the very Word of God, inasmuch as the manuscripts do convey to us the complete vital truth of the originals.

The further affirmation of article X is that copies and translations of Scripture are the Word of God to the extent that they faithfully represent the original. Though we do not actually possess the originals, we have such well-reconstructed translations and copies that to the extent to which they do correspond to the original documents they may be said to be the Word of God. But because of the evident presence of copy errors and errors of translation the distinction must be made between the original work of inspiration in the autographs and the human labor of translating and copying those autographs.

The denial has in view the important point that in those minuscule segments of existing manuscripts where textual criticism has not been able to ascertain with absolute certainty what the original reading was, no essential article of the Christian faith is affected.

To limit inerrancy or inspiration to the original manuscripts does not make the whole contention irrelevant. It does make a difference. If the original text were errant, the church would have the option of rejecting the teachings of that errant text. If the original text is inerrant (and the science of textual criticism must be depended upon to reconstruct that inerrant text), we have no legitimate basis for disobeying a mandate of Scripture where the text is not in doubt. For example, if two theologians agreed that the original text was inerrant and if both agreed as to what the present copy taught and further agreed that the present copy was an accurate representation of the original, then it would follow irresistibly that the two men would be under divine obligation to obey that text. If, on the other hand, we asserted that the original manuscripts were possibly errant and the two theologians then agreed as to what the Bible taught and also agreed that the present translation or copy faithfully represented the original, neither would be under moral obligation to submit to the teachings of that possibly errant original. Therein lies the important issue of the relevancy of the character of the original manuscript.

ARTICLE XI: Infallibility

We affirm that Scripture, having been given by divine inspiration, is infallible, so that, far from misleading us, it is true and reliable in all the matters it addresses. We deny that it is possible for the Bible to be at the same time infallible and errant in its assertions. Infallibility and inerrancy may be distinguished, but not separated.

The central affirmation of article XI is the infallibility of Scripture. Infallibility is defined in this context in positive terms as implying the truthfulness and reliability of all matters that Scripture addresses. Negatively infallibility is defined as the quality of that which does not mislead.

The denial of article XI touches a very important point of controversy, particularly in the modern era. There are those who maintain that the Bible is infallible but not inerrant. Thus, infallibility is separated from inerrancy. The denial argues that it is not possible to maintain with consistency that something is at the same time infallible and errant in its assertions. To maintain such a disjunction

149

between infallibility and inerrancy would involve a glaring contradiction.

Though the words *infallible* and *inerrant* have often been used interchangeably and virtually as synonyms in our language, nevertheless there remains a historic, technical distinction between the two words. *Infallibility* has to do with the question of ability or potential. That which is infallible is said to be unable to make mistakes or to err. The distinction here between that definition of *infallible* and the definition of *inerrant* is the distinction between the potential and the actual, the hypothetical and the real. That which is inerrant is that which, in fact, does not err. Again, theoretically, something may be fallible and at the same time inerrant. That is, it would be possible for someone to err who in fact does not err. However, the reverse is not true. If someone is infallible, that means he cannot err; and if he cannot err, then he does not err. To assert that something is infallible yet at the same time errant is either to distort the meaning of *infallible* and/or *errant*, or else to be in a state of confusion. Thus, *infallibility* and *inerrancy* in this sense cannot be separated though they may indeed be distinguished in terms of meaning. But anything that is infallible, that is, incapable of erring, cannot at the same time err. For if it errs, it proves that it is capable of erring and therefore is not infallible.

In situations where *infallibility* has been substituted for *inerrancy*, it has usually been designed to articulate a lower view of Scripture than that indicated by the word *inerrant*. In fact, however, the term *infallibility* in its original and technical meaning is a higher term than the term *inerrant*. Again, it is important to see that something which is fallible could theoretically be inerrant. But that which is infallible could not theoretically be at the same time errant.

ARTICLE XII: Inerrancy of the Whole

We affirm that Scripture in its entirety is inerrant, being free from all falsehood, fraud, or deceit. *We deny* that biblical infallibility and inerrancy are limited to spiritual, religious or redemptive themes, exclusive of assertions in the fields of history and science. We further deny that scientific hypotheses about earth history may properly be used to overturn the teaching of Scripture on creation and the flood.

Article XII affirms clearly and unambiguously the inerrancy of sacred Scripture. In the affirmation, the meaning of *inerrancy* is given in negative terms: that which is inerrant is "free from falsehood, fraud, or deceit." Here inerrancy is defined by the way of negation, by establishing parameters beyond which we may not move, boundaries we may not transgress. An inerrant Scripture cannot contain falsehood, fraud, or deceit in its teachings or assertions.

The denial explicitly rejects the tendency of some to limit infallibility and inerrancy to specific segments of the biblical message, such as spiritual, religious, or redemptive themes, excluding assertions from the fields of history or science. It has been fashionable in certain quarters to maintain that the Bible is not normal history, but is redemptive history with the accent on redemption. Theories are then established that would limit inspiration to the redemptive theme of redemptive history, allowing the historical dimension of redemptive history to be errant. However, the fact that the Bible is not written like other forms of history does not negate the historical dimension with which it is intimately involved. Though the Bible is indeed *redemptive* history, it is also redemptive *history*, and this means that the acts of salvation wrought by God actually occurred in the space-time world.

With respect to matters of science, the further denial that scientific hypotheses about earth history may be used to overturn the teaching of Scripture on such matters of creation and the flood again rejects the idea that the Bible speaks merely in areas of spiritual value or concerning redemptive themes. The Bible does have something to say about the origin of the earth, about the advent of man, about creation, and about such matters that have scientific import, as the question of the flood. It is important to note that the second denial, that scientific hypotheses about earth history may not be used to overturn the teaching of Scripture on matters such as the creation and the flood, does not carry with it the implication that scientific hypotheses or scientific research are useless to the student of the Bible or that science never has anything to contribute to an understanding of biblical material. It merely denies that the actual teaching of Scripture can be overturned by teachings from external sources.

To illustrate the intention of the second denial of article XII, recall the classic example of the church's debate with the scientific community in the Middle Ages over the question of geocentricity and heliocentricity. The church had adopted the ancient Ptolemaic view that the earth was the center of the universe. Hence, the concept of geocentricity. Scientific inquiry and studies, particularly attending the advent of the telescope, led many scholars to believe that the sun, not the earth, was the center at least of our solar system, for the evidence from the scientific community for the centrality of the sun rather than the earth was seen to be compelling and overwhelming. We remember with embarrassment that Galileo was condemned as a heretic for asserting heliocentricity against what the church believed to be the teaching of Scripture. However, the scientific discoveries made it necessary for the church to reexamine the teaching of Scripture to see whether or not Scripture actually taught geocentricity or if this was an inference read into the Scripture on the basis of an earlier world view. Upon reexamining what Scripture really taught, the church came to the conclusion that there was no real conflict with science on this question of geocentricity because the Bible did not in fact in any place explicitly teach or assert that the earth was the center of either the solar system or the universe. Here the advances of science helped the church to correct an earlier misinterpretation of Scripture. To say that science cannot overturn the teaching of Scripture is not to say that science cannot aid the church in understanding Scripture, or even correct false inferences drawn from Scripture or actual misinterpretations of the Scripture. On the other hand, this does not give one license arbitrarily to reinterpret Scripture to force it into conformity to secular theories of origins or the like. For example, if the secular community asserts that the origin of humanity is the result of a cosmic accident or the product of blind, impersonal forces, such a view cannot possibly be reconciled with the biblical view of the purposive act of God's creation of mankind without doing radical violence to the Bible itself.

153

Questions of the extent of the flood or the literary genre of the earlier chapters of Genesis are not answered by this statement. Questions of biblical interpretation that touch on the field of hermeneutics remain for further investigation and discussion. What the Scriptures actually teach about creation and the flood is not spelled out by this article; but it does spell out that whatever the Bible teaches about creation and the flood cannot be negated by secular theories.

9

THE WORD OF GOD
AND TRUTH

he meaning of *truth* should be self-evident, but this has not been the case where discussions of the truthfulness of the Bible are concerned. What is truth? Some have argued that the Bible is not truthful unless it conforms to modern standards of scientific precision—no round numbers, precise grammar, scientific descriptions of natural phenomena, and so forth. Others have taken an entirely opposite view, arguing that the Bible is truthful so long as it attains its general spiritual ends, regardless of whether it actually makes false statements. Articles XIII–XV thread their way between these extremes. They maintain that the Bible is to be evaluated by its own principles of truth, which do not necessarily include modern forms of scientific expression, but argue at the same time that the statements of Scripture are always without error and, therefore, do not mislead the reader in any way.

Article XIV deals with the way apparent discrepancies—involving problems not yet resolved—should be handled.

ARTICLE XIII: Truth

*We **affirm** the propriety of using* inerrancy *as a theological term with reference to the complete truthfulness of Scripture. We **deny** that it is proper to evaluate Scripture according to standards of truth and error that are alien to its usage or purpose. We further deny that inerrancy is negated by biblical phenomena such as a lack of modern technical precision, irregularities of grammar or spelling, observational descriptions of nature, the reporting of falsehoods, the use of hyperbole and round numbers, the topical arrangement of material, variant selections of material in parallel accounts, or the use of free citations.*

With the combination of the affirmation and denial of article XIII regarding the term *inerrancy*, it may seem to some that, in view of all the qualifications that are listed in the denial, this word is no longer a useful or appropriate term to use with respect to the Bible. Some have said that it has "suffered the death of a thousand qualifications." The same, of course, could be said about the word *God*. Because of the complexity of our concept of God, it has become necessary to qualify in great detail the differences in what is being affirmed and what is being denied when we use the term *God*. Such qualifications do not negate the value of the word but only serve to sharpen its precision and usefulness.

It is important to note that the word *inerrancy* is called a theological term by article XIII. It is an appropriate theological term to refer to the complete truthfulness of Scripture. That is basically what is being asserted with the term

inerrancy: that the Bible is completely true, that all its affirmations and denials correspond with reality. Theological
terms other than inerrancy are frequently in need of qualification and cannot be taken in a crass, literal sense. For
example, the term *omnipotence*, when used to refer to God,
does not literally mean what it may seem to. That is, omnipotence does not mean that God can do anything. The
omnipotence of God does not mean that God can lie or that
God could die or that God could be God and not God at
the same time and in the same relationship. Nevertheless,
as a term that has reference to God's complete sovereign
control and authority over the created world, *omnipotence* is
a perfectly useful and appropriate term in our theological
vocabulary.

Because the term *inerrancy* must be qualified, some have
thought that it would be better to exclude it from the
church's vocabulary. However, the qualifications of the term
are not new nor are they particularly cumbersome, and the
word serves as an appropriate safeguard from those who
would attack the truthfulness of Scripture in subtle ways.
When we speak of inerrancy, then, we are speaking of the
fact that the Bible does not violate its own principles of truth.
This does not mean that the Bible is free from grammatical irregularities or the like, but that it does not contain
assertions which are in conflict with objective reality.

The first denial that "the Bible ought not to be evaluated
according to standards of truth and error alien to its own
use or purpose" indicates that it would be inappropriate to
evaluate the Bible's internal consistency with its own truth
claims by standards foreign to the Bible's own view of truth.
When we say that the truthfulness of Scripture ought to be

evaluated according to its own standards, that means that for the Scripture to be true to its claim it must have an internal consistency compatible with the biblical concept of truth and that all the claims of the Bible must correspond with reality, whether that reality is historical, factual, or spiritual.

The second denial gives us a list of qualifications that is not intended to be exhaustive but rather illustrative of the type of considerations which must be kept in mind when one seeks to define the word *inerrancy*.

Modern technical precision. Inerrancy is not vitiated by the fact, for example, that the Bible occasionally uses round numbers. To say that truth has been distorted when, for example, the size of a crowd or the size of an army is estimated in round numbers would be to impose a criterion of truth that is foreign to the literature under examination. When a newspaper even in modern times says that 50,000 people assembled for a football game, they are not considered to be engaging in falsehood, fraud, or deceit because they have rounded off a number of 49,878, for example, to 50,000. It is an appropriate use of quantitative measurement in historical reporting that does not involve falsehood.

Irregularities of grammar or spelling. Though it is more beautiful and attractive to speak the truth with a fluent style and proper grammar, grammatical correctness is not necessary for the expression of truth. For example, if a man were on trial for murder and was asked if he killed his wife on February 13, and replied "I ain't killed nobody never," the crudity of his grammar would have nothing to do with the truth or falsehood of his statement. He can hardly be convicted of murder because his plea of innocence was couched within the context of rough and "errant" grammar. Inerrancy is not related to the grammatical propriety or impropriety of the language of Scripture.

Observational descriptions of nature. With respect to natural phenomena, it is clear that the Bible speaks from the perspective of the observer on many occasions. The Bible speaks of the sun rising and setting and of the sun moving across the heavens. From the perspective of common observation, it is perfectly appropriate to describe things as they appear to the human eye. To accuse the Bible of planetary motion would again be to impose a foreign perspective and criterion on the Scriptures. No one is offended when the weatherman speaks of sunrises and sunsets. No one accuses the weather bureau of seeking to revert to a medieval perspective of geocentricity or of falsifying the weather forecast by speaking of sunsets and sunrises. Those terms are perfectly appropriate to describe things as they appear to the observer.

The reporting of falsehoods. Some have maintained that the Bible is not inerrant because it reports falsehoods such as the lies of Satan and the fraudulent teachings of false prophets. However, though the Bible does, in fact, contain false statements, they are reported as being lies and falsehoods. So this in no way vitiates the truth value of the biblical record but only enhances it.

The use of hyperbole. The use of hyperbole has been appealed to as a technical reason for rejecting inerrancy. However, hyperbole is a perfectly legitimate literary device. Hyperbole involves the intentional exaggeration of a statement to make a point. It provides the weight of intensity and emphasis that would otherwise be lacking. That the

Bible uses hyperbole is without doubt. That hyperbole vitiates inerrancy is denied. The framers of the document maintain that the use of hyperbole is perfectly consistent with the
Bible's own view of truth.

Other matters, such as the topical arrangement of material, the use of free citations (for example, from the Old Testament by the New Testament writers), and various selections of material and parallel accounts, where different
writers include some information that other writers do not
have and delete some information that others included, in
no way destroy the truthfulness of what is being reported.
Though biblical writers may have arranged their material
differently, they do not affirm that Jesus said on one occasion what he never said on that occasion. Neither are they
claiming that another parallel account is wrong for not
including what they themselves include. As an itinerant
preacher Jesus no doubt said many similar things on different occasions.

By biblical standards of truth and error is meant the view
used both in the Bible and in everyday life, viz., a correspondence view of truth. This part of the article is directed
toward those who would redefine truth to relate merely to
redemptive intent, the purely personal, or the like, rather
than to mean that which corresponds with reality. For example, when Jesus affirmed that Jonah was in "the belly of the
great fish," this statement is true, not simply because of the
redemptive significance the story of Jonah has, but also
because it is literally and historically true. The same may be
said of the New Testament assertions about Adam, Moses,
David, and other Old Testament persons as well as about
Old Testament events.

ARTICLE XIV: Consistency

We affirm the unity and internal consistency of Scripture. *We deny* that alleged errors and discrepancies that have not yet been resolved vitiate the truth claims of the Bible.

Because the Bible is the Word of God and reflects his truthful character, it is important to affirm that it is one. Though it contains much information of a wide diversity of scope and interest, nevertheless there is an internal unity and consistency to the Word of God that flows from the nature of God's truth. God's truthfulness brings unity out of diversity. God is not an author of incoherency or of contradiction. His Word is consistent as well as coherent.

The denial in article XIV deals with the particular problems of harmonization between texts that appear to be contradictory and of a number of other alleged errors and discrepancies pointed out repeatedly by critics. It must be acknowledged that there are some as yet unresolved apparent discrepancies in Scripture. A great deal of careful scrutiny has been applied to the investigation of these, and that effort has yielded very positive results. A great many alleged contradictions have been resolved, some in the early church and others more recently. The trend has been in the direction of reducing problems rather than increasing them. New knowledge acquired about the ancient texts and the meaning of language in the biblical age, as well as new discoveries coming from manuscripts and parchments uncovered by archaeology, have given substantial help in resolving problems and have provided a solid basis for optimism with respect to future resolution of remaining difficulties. Difficulties that have not been resolved may yet be resolved under further scrutiny. This approach to the question of the resolution of difficulties may seem at first glance to be an exercise in "special pleading." However, if any work deserves special consideration it is sacred Scripture. Before we jump to the conclusion that we are faced with an ultimately unresolvable contradiction we must exhaust all possible illuminating research. A spirit of humility demands that we give careful attention to the resolutions that have already been made, and that we acknowledge that we have not as yet left every stone unturned in our efforts to give a fair and judicious hearing to the text of the Bible. Some of the greatest discoveries that have helped us to understand the Bible have come about because we have been forced to dig more deeply in our efforts to reconcile difficulties within the text. It should not be deemed strange that a volume that included sixty-six different books written over one thousand four hundred years would have some difficulties of harmonization within it.

It has often been charged that the Bible is *full* of contradictions. Such statements are unwarranted by the evidence. The amount of seriously difficult passages compared to the total quantity of material found there is very small indeed. It would be injudicious and even foolhardy for us to ignore the truth claims of the Bible simply because of presently unresolved difficulties. We have a parallel here with the presence of anomalies in the scientific world. Anomalies may indeed be so significant that they make it necessary for scientists to rethink their theories about the nature of geology, biology, or the like. For the most part, however, when an overwhelming weight of evidence points to the viability of a theory and some anomalies remain that do not seem to fit the theory, it is not the accepted practice in the scientific world to "scrap" the whole well-attested theory because of a few difficulties that have not yet been resolved. With this analogy in science we may be bold to say that when we approach Scripture as we do, we do nothing more or less than apply the scientific method to our research of Scripture itself.

Every student of Scripture must face squarely and with honesty the difficulties that are still unresolved. To do this demands our deepest intellectual endeavors. We should seek to learn from Scripture as we examine the text again and again. The unresolved difficulties, in the process of being resolved, often yield light to us as we gain a deeper understanding of the Word of God.

ARTICLE XV: Accommodation

We affirm that the doctrine of inerrancy is grounded in the teaching of the Bible about inspiration. *We deny* that Jesus' teaching about Scripture may be dismissed by appeals to accommodation or to any natural limitation of His humanity.

In the affirmation of article XV, inerrancy as a doctrine is viewed as being inseparably related to the biblical teaching on inspiration. Though the Bible nowhere uses the word *inerrancy*, the concept is found in the Scriptures. The Scriptures have their own claim to being the Word of God. The words of the prophets are prefaced by the statement, "Thus sayeth the Lord." Jesus speaks of the Scriptures of the Old Testament as being incapable of being broken (John 10:35). He says that not a jot or tittle of the law will pass away until all be fulfilled (Matt. 5:18). Paul tells us that all is given by inspiration (2 Tim. 3:16). Inerrancy is a corollary of inspiration inasmuch as it is unthinkable that God should inspire that which is fraudulent, false, or deceitful. Thus, though the word *inerrancy* is not explicitly used in the Scriptures, the word *inspired* is, and the concept of inerrancy is designed to do justice to the concept of inspiration.

It should not be thought that because the Bible does not contain the terms *inerrant* or *inerrancy* there is, therefore, no biblical basis for the doctrine of inerrancy. The Bible nowhere uses the term *trinity*, and yet the doctrine of the trinity is clearly taught throughout the New Testament. When the church affirms a doctrine, it finds no necessity to discover a verbal parallel between the doctrine and the words of the Bible itself. What is implied by the affirmation of this article is that the doctrine of the inerrancy of Scripture is a doctrine ultimately based upon the teaching of Jesus himself. The framers of this confession wish to express no higher nor lower view of Scripture than that held and taught by Jesus. That becomes explicit in the denial. The denial expresses that Jesus' teaching about Scripture may not be easily dismissed. It has been fashionable in recent Protestantism to grant that Jesus did indeed hold and teach a doctrine of inspiration that would comport with the concept of inerrancy, but then to argue at the same time that Jesus' view is deficient in light of limitations tied to his human nature. The fact that Jesus held a view of inspiration such as he did is "excused" on the basis that, touching his human nature, Jesus was a product of his times. Jesus, it is urged, could not possibly have known all of the problems that have since been raised by higher criticism. As a result, Jesus, like the rest of his contemporaries, accepted uncritically the prevailing notion of Scripture of his own day. For example, when Jesus mentions that Moses wrote of him, he was unaware of the documentary hypothesis which would apparently demolish any serious case for Mosaic authorship of the first five books of the Old Testament.

From a Protestant perspective, such ignorance by Jesus concerning the truth about Scripture is excused on the basis that the only way he could have known the truth would be for him in his human nature to be omniscient. Now for Jesus in his human nature to be omniscient, that is to know all things, would involve a confusion of the divine and the human natures. Omniscience is an attribute of deity, not of humanity. Since, ordinarily, Protestants do not believe that Jesus' human nature was deified with such attributes as omniscience, it appears perfectly understandable and excusable that in his lack of knowledge he made mistakes about the Scripture. This is the line of reasoning which the denial part of the article disallows.

The problems raised by these explanations are too numerous and too profound for a detailed treatment here. But the point is this: Even though we admit that Jesus in his human nature was not omniscient, we do urge that his claims to teach nothing by his own authority but by the authority of the Father (John 8:28) and to be the very incarnation of truth (John 14:6) would be fraudulent claims if anything that he taught were in error. Even if his error arose out of his ignorance, he would be guilty of sin for claiming to know truth that he in fact did not know. At stake here is our very redemption. For if Jesus taught falsely while claiming to be speaking the truth, he would be guilty of sin. If he were guilty of sin, then obviously his atonement could not atone for himself, let alone for his people. Ultimately, the doctrine of Scripture is bound up with the doctrine of Jesus Christ. It is because of Jesus' high view of Scripture that the framers of this confession so strenuously maintain the high view of Scripture today.

Again, it is fashionable in many circles to believe Jesus when he speaks of heavenly matters, matters of redemption and salvation, but to correct Jesus when he speaks of historical matters such as the writing of the Pentateuch and other matters relating to the doctrine of Scripture. At this point those who accept Jesus when he speaks redemptively but reject him when he speaks historically violate a teaching principle that Jesus himself espoused. Jesus raised the rhetorical question, "How can you believe me concerning heavenly things when you cannot believe me concerning earthly things?" (John 3:12). It seems that we have a generation of scholars who are willing to believe Jesus concerning heavenly matters while rejecting those things which he taught about the earth. (What Jesus says concerning history may be falsified by critical methods, but what he says concerning heavenly matters is beyond the reach of verification or falsification.) The framers of this confession believe that Jesus' principle of the trustworthiness of his teaching as affecting both heavenly matters and earthly matters must be maintained even to this day.

10

THE WORD OF GOD AND YOU

iscussion of inerrancy is merely an academic exercise unless it concerns the individual Christian on the level of his growth in God. But this is precisely what it does. Confession of the full authority and inerrancy of Scripture should lead us to increasing conformity to the image of Christ, which is the God-ordained goal of every Christian. The final articles of affirmation and denial deal with this matter, including the work of the Holy Spirit in helping the believer to understand and apply the Scriptures to his or her life.

ARTICLE XVI: Church History

*We **affirm** that the doctrine of inerrancy has been integral to the church's faith throughout its history. We **deny** that inerrancy is a doctrine invented by scholastic Protestantism, or is a reactionary position postulated in response to negative higher criticism.*

This affirmation again speaks of the doctrine of inerrancy, not the word *inerrancy*. It is readily acknowledged that the word *inerrancy* was not used with any degree of frequency and perhaps not even at all before the seventeenth century. For example, Martin Luther nowhere uses the term *inerrancy* as a noun with respect to Scripture. Because of this some have said that Luther did not believe in inerrancy, but Luther argued that the Scriptures never "err." To say that the Scriptures never err is to say nothing more nor less than that the Bible is inerrant. So though the word *inerrancy* is of relatively modern invention, the concept is rooted not only in the biblical witness to Scripture itself but also in the acceptance of the vast majority of God's people throughout the history of the Christian church. We find the doctrine taught, embraced, and espoused by men such as Augustine, Thomas Aquinas, Martin Luther, John Calvin, Jonathan Edwards, John Wesley, and a host of Christian scholars and teachers throughout the history of the church. While the language of inerrancy does not appear in Protestant confessions of faith until the modern ages, the concept of inerrancy is surely not foreign or strange to the confessions of East or West, Catholic or Protestant.

The denial follows the thinking of the affirmation closely. The denial is simply that inerrancy as a concept is not the product of a rigid, sterile, rationalistic approach to Scripture born of the scholastic movement of seventeenth-century Protestantism. Nor is it proper to understand the doctrine as a twentieth-century reaction to liberal theology or "modernism."

It is not the affirmation of inerrancy that is of recent vintage; it is its denial. It is not the reaction to higher criticism that is new, but it is uncritically accepted philosophical assumptions of negative criticism that is a new phenomenon in mainline Christianity. Such criticism is not new in the sense that no one ever questioned the integrity or authenticity of Scripture in past ages, but the newness of the phenomenon is its widespread and easy acceptance within churches and by leaders who would claim allegiance to mainline Christianity.

ARTICLE XVII: Witness of the Spirit

We affirm that the Holy Spirit bears witness to the Scriptures, assuring believers of the truthfulness of God's written Word. *We deny* that this witness of the Holy Spirit operates in isolation from or against Scripture.

Article XVII attests to the doctrine of the internal testimony of the Holy Spirit. That is to say, our personal conviction of the truth of Scripture rests not on the external evidences to the Scripture's truthfulness in and of themselves, but those evidences are confirmed in our hearts by the special work of God the Holy Spirit. The Spirit himself bears witness to our human spirit that the Scriptures are indeed the Word of God. Here God himself confirms the truthfulness of his own Word.

The denial guards against substituting a reliance upon the immediate guidance of the Holy Spirit for the content of Scripture itself. The thought behind the denial is that the Holy Spirit normally works in conjunction with the Scripture and speaks to us through the Scripture, not against the Scripture or apart from the Scripture. Word and Spirit are to be viewed together, Word bearing witness to the Spirit and being the means by which we test the spirits to see if they be of God (1 John 4:1), and the Spirit working within our hearts to confirm the Word of God to our-selves. Thus, there is reciprocity between Word and Spirit, and they are never to be set over against each other.

ARTICLE XVIII: Interpretation

*We **affirm** that the text of Scripture is to be interpreted by grammatico-historical exegesis, taking account of its literary forms and devices, and that Scripture is to interpret Scripture. **We deny** the legitimacy of any treatment of the text or quest for sources lying behind it that leads to relativizing, dehistoricizing, or dis-counting its teaching, or rejecting its claims to authorship.*

Article XVIII touches on some of the most basic prin-ciples of biblical interpretation. Though this article does not spell out in detail a vast comprehensive system of hermeneutics, it nevertheless gives basic guidelines on which the framers of the confession were able to agree. The first is that the text of Scripture is to be interpreted by grammatico-historical exegesis. *Grammatico-historical* is a technical term that refers to the process by which we take the structures and time periods of the written texts seriously as we interpret them. Biblical interpreters are not given the license to spiritualize or allegorize texts against the grammatical structure and form of the text itself. The Bible is not to be reinterpreted to be brought into con-formity with contemporary philosophies but is to be under-stood in its intended meaning and word usage as it was written at the time it was composed. To hold to gram-matico-historical exegesis is to disallow the turning of the Bible into a wax nose that can be shaped and reshaped according to modern conventions of thought. The Bible is to be interpreted as it was written, not reinterpreted as we would like it to have been written according to the prejudices of our own era.

The second principle of the affirmation is that we are to take account of the literary forms and devices that are found within the Scriptures themselves. This goes back to principles of interpretation espoused by Luther and the Reformers. A verb is to be interpreted as a verb; a noun as a noun, a parable as a parable, didactic literature as didactic literature, narrative history as narrative history, poetry as poetry, and the like. To turn narrative history into poetry or poetry into narrative history would be to violate the intended meaning of the text. Thus, it is important for all biblical interpreters to be aware of the literary forms and grammatical structures that are found within the Scripture. An analysis of these forms is proper and appropriate for any correct interpretation of the text.

The third principle in the affirmation is that Scripture is to interpret Scripture. Historically, this principle is called the "analogy of faith." It rests on the previous affirmation that the Bible represents a unified, consistent, and coherent Word from God. Any interpretation of a passage that yields a meaning in direct contradiction to another portion of Scripture is disallowed. It is when Scripture interprets Scripture that the sovereignty of the Holy Spirit, the supreme interpreter of the Bible, is duly acknowledged. Arbitrarily setting one part of Scripture against another would violate this principle. Scripture is to be interpreted therefore in terms not only of its immediate context but also of the whole context of the Word of God.

171

The denial part of article XVIII decries the propriety of critical analyses of the text that produce a relativization of the Bible. This does not prohibit an appropriate quest for literary sources or even oral sources that may be discerned through source criticism but draws a line as to the extent to which such critical analysis can go. When the quest for sources produces a dehistoricizing of the Bible, a rejection of its teaching, or a rejection of the Bible's own claims of authorship, it has trespassed beyond its proper limits. This does not prohibit the external examination of evidence to discover the authorship of books that go unnamed in sacred Scriptures such as the Epistle to the Hebrews. A search is even allowable for literary traditions that may have been brought together by a final editor whose name is mentioned in Scripture. It is never legitimate, however, to run counter to express biblical affirmation.

ARTICLE XIX: Health of the Church

We affirm that a confession of the full authority, infallibility, and inerrancy of Scripture is vital to a sound understanding of the whole of the Christian faith. We further affirm that such confession should lead to increasing conformity to the image of Christ. *We deny* that such confession is necessary for salvation. However, we further deny that inerrancy can be rejected without grave consequences, both to the individual and to the church.

Article XIX's affirmation speaks to the relevance of the doctrine of inerrancy to the life of the Christian. Here the functional character of biblical authority is in view. The article is affirming that the confession is not limited to doctrinal concern for theological purity but originates in a profound concern that the Bible remain the authority for the living out of the Christian life. It also recognizes that it is possible for people to believe in the inerrancy or infallibility of Scripture and lead godless lives. It recognizes that a confession of a doctrine of Scripture is not enough to bring us to sanctification but that it is a very important part of the growth process of the Christian that he should rest his confidence in the truthful revelation of the Word of God and thereby should be moved inwardly to conform to the image of Christ. A strong doctrine of the authority of Scripture should, when properly implemented, lead a person to a greater degree of conformity to that Word he espouses as true.

The denial in article XIX is very important. The framers of the confession are saying unambiguously that confession of belief in the inerrancy of Scripture is not an essential of the Christian faith necessary for salvation. We gladly acknowledge that people who do not hold to this doctrine may be earnest and genuine, zealous, and in many ways dedicated Christians. We do not regard acceptance of inerrancy to be a test for salvation. However, we urge as a committee and as an assembly that people consider the severe consequences that may befall the individual or church which casually and easily rejects inerrancy. We believe that history has demonstrated again and again that there is all too often a close relationship between rejection of inerrancy and subsequent defections from matters of the Christian faith that are essential to salvation. When the church loses its confidence in the authority of sacred Scripture the church inevitably looks to human opinion as its guiding light. When that happens, the purity of the church

173

is direly threatened. Thus, we urge upon our Christian brothers and sisters of all professions and denominations to join with us in a reaffirmation of the full authority, integrity, infallibility, and inerrancy of sacred Scripture to the end that our lives may be brought under the authority of God's Word, that we may glorify Christ in our lives, individually and corporately as the church.

Appendix 1

THE LIGONIER STATEMENT
(1973)

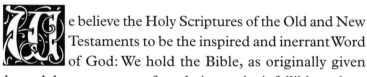e believe the Holy Scriptures of the Old and New Testaments to be the inspired and inerrant Word of God: We hold the Bible, as originally given through human agents of revelation, to be infallible and see this as a crucial article of faith with implications for the entire life and practice of all Christian people. With the great fathers of Christian history we declare our confidence in the total trustworthiness of the Scriptures, urging that any view which imputes to them a lesser degree of inerrancy than total, is in conflict with the Bible's self-testimony in general and with the teaching of Jesus Christ in particular. Out of obedience to the Lord of the Church we submit ourselves unreservedly to his authoritative view of Holy Writ.

Appendix 2

THE CHICAGO STATEMENT ON BIBLICAL INERRANCY

(1978)

he authority of Scripture is a key issue for the Christian church in this and every age. Those who profess faith in Jesus Christ as Lord and Savior are called to show the reality of their discipleship by humbly and faithfully obeying God's written Word. To stray from Scripture in faith or conduct is disloyalty to our Master. Recognition of the total truth and trustworthiness of Holy Scripture is essential to a full grasp and adequate confession of its authority.

The following Statement affirms this inerrancy of Scripture afresh, making clear our understanding of it and warning against its denial. We are persuaded that to deny it is to set aside the witness of Jesus Christ and of the Holy Spirit and to refuse that submission to the claims of God's own Word which marks true Christian faith. We see it as our timely duty to make this affirmation in the face of current lapses from the truth of inerrancy among our fellow Christians and misunderstanding of this doctrine in the world at large.

This Statement consists of three parts: a Summary Statement, Articles of Affirmation and Denial, and an accompanying Exposition. It has been prepared in the course of a three-day consultation in Chicago. Those who have signed the Summary Statement and the Articles wish to affirm their own conviction as to the inerrancy of Scripture and to encourage and challenge one another and all Christians to growing appreciation and understanding of this doctrine. We acknowledge the limitations of a document prepared in a brief, intensive conference and do not propose that this Statement be given creedal weight. Yet we rejoice in the deepening of our own convictions through our discussions together, and we pray that the Statement we have signed may be used to the glory of our God toward a new reformation of the church in its faith, life and mission.

We offer this Statement in a spirit, not of contention, but of humility and love, which we purpose by God's grace to maintain in any future dialogue arising out of what we have said. We gladly acknowledge that many who deny the inerrancy of Scripture do not display the consequences of this denial in the rest of their belief and behavior, and we are conscious that we who confess this doctrine often deny it in life by failing to bring our thoughts and deeds, our traditions and habits, into true subjection to the divine Word.

We invite response to this statement from any who see reason to amend its affirmations about Scripture by the light of Scripture itself, under whose infallible authority we stand as we speak. We claim no personal infallibility for the witness we bear, and for any help which enables us to strengthen this testimony to God's Word we shall be grateful.

A Short Statement

1. God, who is Himself truth and speaks truth only, has inspired Holy Scripture in order thereby to reveal Himself to lost mankind through Jesus Christ as Creator and Lord, Redeemer and Judge. Holy Scripture is God's witness to Himself.

2. Holy Scripture, being God's own Word, written by men prepared and superintended by His Spirit, is of infallible divine authority in all matters upon which it touches: it is to be believed, as God's instruction, in all that it affirms; obeyed, as God's command, in all that it requires; embraced, as God's pledge, in all that it promises.

3. The Holy Spirit, Scripture's divine author, both authenticates it to us by His inward witness and opens our minds to understand its meaning.

4. Being wholly and verbally God-given, Scripture is without error or fault in all its teaching, no less in what it states about God's acts in creation, about the events of world history, and about its own literary origins under God, than in its witness to God's saving grace in individual lives.

5. The authority of Scripture is inescapably impaired if this total divine inerrancy is in any way limited or disregarded, or made relative to a view of truth

179

contrary to the Bible's own; and such lapses bring serious loss to both the individual and the church.

Articles of Affirmation and Denial

Article I

We affirm that the Holy Scriptures are to be received as the authoritative Word of God.

We deny that the Scriptures receive their authority from the church, tradition, or any other human source.

Article II

We affirm that the Scriptures are the supreme written norm by which God binds the conscience, and that the authority of the church is subordinate to that of Scripture.

We deny that church creeds, councils, or declarations have authority greater than or equal to the authority of the Bible.

Article III

We affirm that the written Word in its entirety is revelation given by God.

We deny that the Bible is merely a witness to revelation, or only becomes revelation in encounter, or depends on the responses of men for its validity.

180

Article IV

We affirm that God who made mankind in His image has used language as a means of revelation.

We deny that human language is so limited by our creatureliness that it is rendered inadequate as a vehicle for divine revelation. We further deny that the corruption of human culture and language through sin has thwarted God's work of inspiration.

Article V

We affirm that God's revelation within the Holy Scriptures was progressive.

We deny that later revelation, which may fulfill earlier revelation, ever corrects or contradicts it. We further deny that any normative revelation has been given since the completion of the New Testament writings.

Article VI

We affirm that the whole of Scripture and all its parts, down to the very words of the original, were given by divine inspiration.

We deny that the inspiration of Scripture can rightly be affirmed of the whole without the parts, or of some parts but not the whole.

Article VII

We affirm that inspiration was the work in which God by His Spirit, through human writers, gave us His

Word. The origin of Scripture is divine. The mode of divine inspiration remains largely a mystery to us.

We deny that inspiration can be reduced to human insight, or to heightened states of consciousness of any kind.

Article VIII

We affirm that God in His work of inspiration utilized the distinctive personalities and literary styles of the writers whom He had chosen and prepared.

We deny that God, in causing these writers to use the very words that He chose, overrode their personalities.

Article IX

We affirm that inspiration, though not conferring omniscience, guaranteed true and trustworthy utterance on all matters of which the biblical authors were moved to speak and write.

We deny that the finitude or fallenness of these writers, by necessity or otherwise, introduced distortion or falsehood into God's Word.

Article X

We affirm that inspiration, strictly speaking, applies only to the autographic text of Scripture, which in the providence of God can be ascertained from available manuscripts with great accuracy. We further affirm that copies and translations of Scripture are the Word of God to the extent that they faithfully represent the original.

We deny that any essential element of the Christian faith is affected by the absence of the autographs. We further deny that this absence renders the assertion of biblical inerrancy invalid or irrelevant.

Article XI

We affirm that Scripture, having been given by divine inspiration, is infallible, so that, far from misleading us, it is true and reliable in all the matters it addresses.

We deny that it is possible for the Bible to be at the same time infallible and errant in its assertions. Infallibility and inerrancy may be distinguished, but not separated.

Article XII

We affirm that Scripture in its entirety is inerrant, being free from all falsehood, fraud, or deceit.

We deny that biblical infallibility and inerrancy are limited to spiritual, religious, or redemptive themes, exclusive of assertions in the fields of history and science. We further deny that scientific hypotheses about earth history may properly be used to overturn the teaching of Scripture on creation and the flood.

Article XIII

We affirm the propriety of using *inerrancy* as a theological term with reference to the complete truthfulness of Scripture.

We deny that it is proper to evaluate Scripture according to standards of truth and error that are alien to its usage or purpose. We further deny that inerrancy is negated by biblical phenomena such as a lack of modern technical precision, irregularities of grammar or spelling, observational descriptions of nature, the reporting of falsehoods, the use of hyperbole and round numbers, the topical arrangement of material, variant selections of material in parallel accounts, or the use of free citations.

Article XIV

We affirm the unity and internal consistency of Scripture.

We deny that alleged errors and discrepancies that have not yet been resolved vitiate the truth claims of the Bible.

Article XV

We affirm that the doctrine of inerrancy is grounded in the teaching of the Bible about inspiration.

We deny that Jesus' teaching about Scripture may be dismissed by appeals to accommodation or to any natural limitation of His humanity.

Article XVI

We affirm that the doctrine of inerrancy has been integral to the church's faith throughout its history.

We deny that inerrancy is a doctrine invented by scholastic Protestantism, or is a reactionary position postulated in response to negative higher criticism.

Article XVII

We affirm that the Holy Spirit bears witness to the Scriptures, assuring believers of the truthfulness of God's written Word.

We deny that this witness of the Holy Spirit operates in isolation from or against Scripture.

Article XVIII

We affirm that the text of Scripture is to be interpreted by grammatico-historical exegesis, taking account of its literary forms and devices, and that Scripture is to interpret Scripture.

We deny the legitimacy of any treatment of the text or quest for sources lying behind it that leads to relativizing, dehistoricizing, or discounting its teaching, or rejecting its claims to authorship.

Article XIX

We affirm that a confession of the full authority, infallibility, and inerrancy of Scripture is vital to a sound understanding of the whole of the Christian faith. We further affirm that such confession should lead to increasing conformity to the image of Christ.

We deny that such confession is necessary for salvation. However, we further deny that inerrancy can be rejected without grave consequences, both to the individual and to the church.

Exposition

Our understanding of the doctrine of inerrancy must be set in the context of the broader teachings of the Scripture concerning itself. This exposition gives an account of the outline of doctrine from which our summary statement and articles are drawn.

Creation, Revelation and Inspiration

The triune God, who formed all things by His creative utterances and governs all things by his Word of decree, made mankind in His own image for a life of communion with Himself, on the model of the eternal fellowship of loving communication within the Godhead. As God's image-bearer, man was to hear God's word addressed to him and to respond in the joy of adoring obedience. Over and above God's self-disclosure in the created order and the sequence of events within it, human beings from Adam on have received verbal messages from Him, either directly, as stated in Scripture, or indirectly in the form of part or all of Scripture itself.

When Adam fell, the Creator did not abandon mankind to final judgment but promised salvation and began to reveal Himself as Redeemer in a sequence of historical events centering on Abraham's family and culminating in the life, death, resurrection, present heavenly ministry, and promised return of Jesus Christ. Within this frame God has from time to time spoken specific words of judgment and mercy, promise and command, to sinful human beings so drawing them into a covenant relation of mutual commitment between Him and them in which He blesses them with gifts of grace and they bless Him in responsive adoration. Moses, whom God used as mediator to carry His words to His people at the time of the Exodus, stands at the head of a long line of prophets in whose mouths and writings God put His words for delivery to Israel. God's purpose in this succession of messages was to maintain his covenant by causing his people to know His name—that is, His nature—and His will both of precept and purpose in the present and for the future. This line of prophetic spokesmen from God came to completion in Jesus Christ, God's incarnate Word, who was Himself a prophet—more than a prophet, but not less—and in the apostles and prophets of the first Christian generation. When God's final and climactic message, His word to the world concerning Jesus Christ, had been spoken and elucidated by those in the apostolic circle, the sequence of revealed messages ceased. Henceforth, the church was to live and know God by what He had already said, and said for all time.

At Sinai God wrote the terms of His Covenant on tables of stone, as His enduring witness and for lasting accessibility, and throughout the period of prophetic and apostolic revelation He prompted men to write the messages given to and through them, along with celebratory records of His dealings with His people, plus moral reflections on covenant life and forms of praise and prayer for covenant mercy. The theological reality of inspiration in the producing of biblical documents corresponds to that of spoken prophecies: although the human writers' personalities were expressed in what they wrote, the words were divinely constituted. Thus, what Scripture says, God says; its authority is His authority, for He is its ultimate Author, having given it through the minds and words of chosen and prepared men who in freedom and faithfulness "spoke from God as they were carried along by the Holy Spirit" (2 Peter 1:21). Holy Scripture must be acknowledged as the Word of God by virtue of its divine origin.

Authority: Christ and the Bible

Jesus Christ, the Son of God who is the Word made flesh, our Prophet, Priest, and King, is the ultimate Mediator of God's communication to man, as He is of all God's gifts of grace. The revelation He gave was more than verbal; He revealed the Father by His presence and His deeds as well. Yet His words were crucially important; for He was God, He spoke from the Father, and His words will judge all men at the Last Day.

As the prophesied Messiah, Jesus Christ is the central theme of Scripture. The Old Testament looked ahead to Him; the New Testament looks back to His first coming and on to His second. Canonical Scripture is the divinely inspired and therefore normative witness to Christ. No hermeneutic, therefore, of which the historical Christ is not the focal point is acceptable. Holy Scripture must be treated as what it essentially is—the witness of the Father to the incarnate Son.

It appears that the Old Testament canon had been fixed by the time of Jesus. The New Testament canon is likewise now closed inasmuch as no new apostolic witness to the historical Christ can now be borne. No new revelation (as distinct from Spirit-given understanding of existing revelation) will be given until Christ comes again. The canon was created in principle by divine inspiration. The church's part was to discern the canon which God had created, not to devise one of its own.

The word *canon*, signifying a rule or standard, is a pointer to authority, which means the right to rule and control. Authority in Christianity belongs to God in His revelation, which means, on the one hand, Jesus Christ, the living Word, and, on the other hand, Holy Scripture, the written Word. But the authority of Christ and that of Scripture are one. As our Prophet, Christ testified that Scripture cannot be broken. As our Priest and King, He devoted His earthly life to fulfilling the law and the prophets, even dying in obedience to the words of messianic prophecy. Thus, as He saw Scripture attesting Him and His authority, so by His own submission to Scripture He attested its authority. As He bowed to His Father's instruction given in His Bible (our Old Testament), so He requires His disciples to do—not, however, in isolation but in conjunction with the apostolic witness to Himself which He undertook to inspire by His gift of the Holy Spirit. So Christians show themselves faithful servants of their Lord by bowing to the divine instruction given in the prophetic and apostolic writings which together make up our Bible.

By authenticating each other's authority, Christ and Scripture coalesce into a single fount of authority. The biblically interpreted Christ and the Christ-centered, Christ-proclaiming Bible are from this standpoint one. As from the face of inspiration we infer that what Scripture says, God says, so from the revealed relation between Jesus Christ and

Scripture we may equally declare that what Scripture says, Christ says.

Infallibility, Inerrancy, Interpretation

Holy Scripture, as the inspired Word of God witnessing authoritatively to Jesus Christ, may properly be called *infallible* and *inerrant*. These negative terms have a special value, for they explicitly safeguard crucial positive truths.

Infallible signifies the quality of neither misleading nor being misled and so safeguards in categorical terms the truth that Holy Scripture is a sure, safe, and reliable rule and guide in all matters.

Similarly, *inerrant* signifies the quality of being free from all falsehood or mistake and so safeguards the truth that Holy Scripture is entirely true and trustworthy in all its assertions.

We affirm that canonical Scripture should always be interpreted on the basis that it is infallible and inerrant. However, in determining what the God-taught writer is asserting in each passage, we must pay the most careful attention to its claims and character as a human production. In inspiration, God utilized the culture and conventions of His penman's milieu, a milieu that God controls in His sovereign providence; it is misinterpretation to imagine otherwise.

So history must be treated as history, poetry as poetry, hyperbole and metaphor as hyperbole and metaphor, generalization and approximation as what they are, and so forth. Differences between literary conventions in Bible times and in ours must also be observed: since, for instance, nonchronological narration and imprecise citation were conventional and acceptable and violated no expectations in those days, we must not regard these things as faults when we find them in Bible writers. When total precision of a particular kind was not expected nor aimed at, it is no error not to have achieved it. Scripture is inerrant, not in the sense of being absolutely precise by modern standards, but in the sense of making good its claims and achieving that measure of focused truth at which its authors aimed.

The truthfulness of Scripture is not negated by the appearance in it of irregularities of grammar or spelling, phenomenal descriptions of nature, reports of false statements (e.g., the lies of Satan), or seeming discrepancies between one passage and another. It is not right to set the so-called "phenomena" of Scripture against the teaching of Scripture about itself. Apparent inconsistencies should not be ignored. Solution of them, where this can be convincingly achieved, will encourage our faith, and where for the present no convincing solution is at hand we shall significantly honor God by trusting His assurance that His Word is true, despite these appearances, and by maintaining our confidence that one day they will be seen to have been illusions.

Inasmuch as all Scripture is the product of a single divine mind, interpretation must stay within the bounds of the analogy of Scripture and eschew hypotheses that would correct one biblical passage by another, whether in the name of progressive revelation or of the imperfect enlightenment of the inspired writer's mind.

Although Holy Scripture is nowhere culture-bound in the sense that its teaching lacks universal validity, it is sometimes culturally conditioned by the customs and conventional views of a particular period, so that the application of its principles today calls for a different sort of action.

Skepticism and Criticism

Since the Renaissance, and more particularly since the Enlightenment, worldviews have been developed which involve skepticism about basic Christian tenets. Such are the agnosticism which denies that God is knowable, the rationalism which denies that He is incomprehensible, the idealism which denies that He is transcendent, and the existentialism which denies rationality in His relationships with us. When these un- and antibiblical principles seep into men's theologies at a presuppositional level, as today they frequently do, faithful interpretation of Holy Scripture becomes impossible.

Transmission and Translation

Since God has nowhere promised an inerrant transmission of Scripture, it is necessary to affirm that only the autographic text of the original documents was inspired and to maintain the need of textual criticism as a means of detecting any slips that may have crept into the text in the course of its transmission. The verdict of this science, however, is that the Hebrew and Greek text appear to be amazingly well preserved, so that we are amply justified in affirming, with the Westminster Confession, a singular providence of God in this matter and in declaring that the authority of Scripture is in no way jeopardized by the fact that the copies we possess are not entirely error free.

Similarly, no translation is or can be perfect, and all translations are an additional step away from the *autographa*. Yet the verdict of linguistic science is that English-speaking Christians, at least, are exceedingly well served in these days with a host of excellent translations and have no cause for hesitating to conclude that the true Word of God is within their reach. Indeed, in view of the frequent repetition in Scripture of the main matters with which it deals and also of the Holy Spirit's constant witness to and through the Word, no serious translation of Holy Scripture will so destroy its meaning as to render it unable to make its reader "wise for salvation through faith in Christ Jesus" (2 Timothy 3:15).

Inerrancy and Authority

In our affirmation of the authority of Scripture as involving its total truth, we are consciously standing with Christ and His apostles, indeed with the whole Bible and with the main stream of church history from the first days until very recently. We are concerned at the casual, inadvertent, and seemingly thoughtless way in which a belief of such far-reaching importance has been given up by so many in our day.

We are conscious, too, that great and grave confusion results from ceasing to maintain the total truth of the Bible whose authority one professes to acknowledge. The result of taking this step is that the Bible which God gave loses its authority, and what has authority instead is a Bible reduced in content according to the demands of one's critical reasonings and in principle reducible still further once one has started. This means that at bottom independent reason now has authority, as opposed to Scriptural teaching. If this is not seen and if for the time being basic evangelical doctrines are still held, persons denying the full truth of Scripture may claim an evangelical identity while methodologically they have moved away from the evangelical principle of knowledge to an unstable subjectivism, and will find it hard not to move further.

We affirm that what Scripture says, God says. May He be glorified. Amen and Amen.

NOTES

Introduction

1. Benjamin B. Warfield, *The Inspiration and Authority of the Bible*, ed. Samuel G. Craig (Philadelphia: Presbyterian and Reformed, 1948).

2. Ned B. Stonehouse and Paul Wooley, eds. *The Infallible Word* (Philadelphia: Presbyterian and Reformed, 1946).

3. Edward J. Young, *Thy Word Is Truth* (Grand Rapids: Eerdmans, 1957).

4. George Marsden, *Reforming Fundamentalism: Fuller Seminary and the New Evangelicalism* (Grand Rapids: Eerdmans, 1987).

5. For an overview of these developments within evangelicalism, see Iain H. Murray, *Evangelicalism Divided* (Edinburgh: Banner of Truth, 2000).

6. John Warwick Montgomery, ed., *God's Inerrant Word: An International Symposium on the Trustworthiness of Scripture* (Minneapolis: Bethany, 1974).

7. R. C. Sproul, *Explaining Inerrancy* (Orlando: Ligonier Ministries, 1996).

Chapter 1: *Sola Scriptura:* Crucial to Evangelicalism

1. "Die einzige Quelle und Norm aller christlichen Erkenntnis ist die heilige Schrift," a statement in Heinrich Heppe, *Die Dogmatik der evangelisch-reformierten Kirche* (Neukirchen Kreis Moers: Neukirchener, 1958), p. 10.

2. Harold J. Grimm, *The Reformation Era* (New York: Macmillan, 1954), p. 114.

3. Gordon Rupp, *Luther's Progress to the Diet of Worms* (New York: Harper, 1964), p. 69.

4. Paul Althaus, *The Theology of Martin Luther,* trans. Robert C. Schultz (Philadelphia: Fortress, 1966), pp. 6–7. Althaus cites Luther: "But everyone, indeed, knows that at times they [the fathers] have erred as men will; therefore, I am ready to trust them only when they prove their opinions from Scripture, which has never erred" (WA 7:315; LW 32:11). Also: "Hold to Scripture and the Word of God. There you will find truth and security— assurance and a faith that is complete, pure, sufficient, and enduring" (WA 7:455; LW 32:98).

5. This is precisely the challenge raised by Hans Küng. He says: "The counter question to Protestant theology must be: Is it sufficient to replace the infallibility of the ecclesiastical teaching office with the infallibility of the Bible? Instead of the infallibility of the Roman pontiffs or of ecumenical councils, are we to have the infallibility of a 'paper pope'?" Küng's answer is clearly in the negative. Hans Küng, *Infallible? An Inquiry,* trans. Edward Quinn (New York: Doubleday, 1971), p. 209.

6. For a more thorough treatment of Luther's view of inerrancy, see John Warwick Montgomery, "Lessons from Luther on the Inerrancy of Holy Writ," in John Warwick Montgomery, ed., *God's Inerrant Word: An International Symposium on the Trustworthiness of Scripture* (Minneapolis: Bethany, 1974), pp. 63–94. See also J. I. Packer, "Calvin's View of Scripture," in Montgomery, ed., *God's Inerrant Word,* pp. 95–114.

7. The confessional citations are taken from Arthur C. Cochrane, ed., *Reformed Confessions of the Sixteenth Century* (Philadelphia: Westminster, 1966).

8. Cf. French Confession, art. 2; Belgic Confession, art. 2; Second Helvetic Confession, chap. 12; Westminster Confession, chap. 1. A further technical point may be added: General revelation is no less infallible than Scripture. The sola here refers to a unique source of infallible written revelation.

9. *Canons and Decrees of the Council of Trent: Original Text with English Translation,* trans. H. J. Schroeder (St. Louis: Herder, 1941), p. 17. Italics mine.

10. G. C. Berkouwer, *Vatikaans Concilie en Nieuwe Theologie* (Kampen: Kok, 1964), p. 129.

11. Ibid., pp. 110–12.

12. "Haec porro supernaturalis revelation, secundum universalis Ecclesiae fidem a sancta Tridentina Synodo declaratam continetur 'in libris scriptis et sine scripto traditionibus.'" Vatican 1 (Denziger 1787). "Verum quoque est, theologis semper redeundum esse ad divinae revelationis fontes: eorum enim est indicare qua ratione ea quae a vivo Magisterio docentur, in Sacris Litteris et in divina 'traditione,' sive explicite, sive implicite inveniantur." *Humani generis* (Denzinger 2314).

13. " 'Truth, Unity, and Peace,' the Encyclical 'Ad Petri Cathedram' of Pope John XXIII to the Entire Catholic World," in *The Encyclicals and Other Messages of John XXIII* (Washington, D.C.: TPS, 1964), pp. 24ff.

14. Bernard Ramm, "Is 'Scripture Alone' the Essence of Christianity?" in Jack Rogers, ed., *Biblical Authority* (Waco: Word, 1977), pp. 111–12.

15. Ibid., p. 112.

16. One important qualification must be added here. If a person were convinced that Jesus infallibly taught a particular view of Scripture and at the same time obstinately refused to affirm or submit to it, it would properly raise grave questions about the state of his soul.

17. J. I. Packer, " 'Sola Scriptura' in History and Today," in John Warwick Montgomery, ed., *God's Inerrant Word*, p. 44.

18. Ibid., p. 43.

19. Francis Schaeffer, "Form and Freedom in the Church," in J. D. Douglas, ed., *Let the Earth Hear His Voice* (Minneapolis: World Wide, 1975), pp. 364–65. Cited by Richard Lovelace in his unpublished essay "Limited Inerrancy: Some Historical Perspectives."

20. Francis Schaeffer, *No Final Conflict* (Downers Grove, Ill.: InterVarsity, 1975), p. 13.

21. Harold Lindsell, *The Battle for the Bible* (Grand Rapids: Zondervan, 1976), p. 139.

22. Ramm, "Is 'Scripture Alone' the Essence of Christianity?" p. 122.

23. Ibid., pp. 122–23.

24. Though full inerrancy has been a rallying point for much evangelical cooperation, it would be incorrect to assert that historic Evangelicalism has been monolithic in its view of Scripture. In many instances (as in the Evangelical Theological Society) inerrancy has functioned as a strong point of unity. But I am not prepared to maintain that full inerrancy is the *wesen* of (essential to) Evangelicalism in the sense that one cannot be an evangelical if he rejects it. I regard limited inerrancy to be inconsistent with *sola Scriptura* and detrimental to the cause of Evangelicalism, but not the touchstone of Evangelicalism itself.

25. In a book dedicated to Rudolf Bultmann, Van Harvey makes this observation: "Of these many problems, none has caused more consternation and anxiety in the breasts and minds of Christian believers than the application of critical historical methods to the New Testament and, especially, to the life of Jesus. It is fashionable among contemporary Protestant theologians to consider this aspect of the problem something of a dead issue except, that is, among fundamentalists and other conservative Christians. My conviction is that this attribute is unwarranted, that even the most sophisticated theological programs of the last two or three decades have failed to grapple in any rigorous and clear fashion with the thorny issues created by a revolution in the consciousness of Western man of which critical historiography is but the expression." Van Harvey, *The Historian and the Believer* (New York: Macmillan, 1966), p. xi.

26. Paul King Jewett, *Man as Male and Female: A Study in Sexual Relationships from a Theological Point of View* (Grand Rapids: Eerdmans, 1975), pp. 112–35.

27. See *Sexuality and the Human Community* (Philadelphia: Office of the General Assembly of the United Presbyterian Church in the U.S.A., 1970).

Chapter 2: The Establishment of Scripture

1. Benjamin Breckinridge Warfield, *Revelation and Inspiration*, ed. Ethelbert D. Warfield et al. (New York: Oxford University, 1932), p. 451.

2. Ibid., p. 455.

3. G. C. Berkouwer, *De Heilige Schrift*, vol. 1, *Dogmatische Studiën* (Kampen: Kok, 1966), p. 89.

4. Everett F. Harrison, *Introduction to the New Testament* (Grand Rapids: Eerdmans, 1964), p. 112.

5. Ibid., p. 122.

6. R. K. Harrison, *Introduction to the Old Testament: With a Comprehensive Review of Old Testament Studies and a Special Supplement on the Apocrypha* (Grand Rapids: Eerdmans, 1969), p. 262.

7. Francis Turretin, *Institutes of Elenctic Theology*, 3 vols., trans. George Musgrave Giger, ed. James T. Dennison Jr. (Phillipsburg, N.J.: P&R, 1992–1997), 1:102.

8. John Calvin, *Institutes of the Christian Religion*, 2 vols., trans. Henry Beveridge (1845; reprint, Grand Rapids: Eerdmans, 1964), 1:69 (1.7.2).

9. Rudolf Bultmann et al., *Kerygma and Myth: A Theological Debate*, ed. Hans Werner Bartsch, trans. Reginald H. Fuller (New York: Harper & Row, 1961), p. 3.

10. Ibid., pp. 4–5.

11. Berkouwer, *De Heilige Schrift*, 1:93.

Chapter 3: The Case for Inerrancy: A Methodological Analysis

1. G. C. Berkouwer gives particular attention to the papal encyclicals *Providentissimus Deus* (Leo XIII, 1893) and *Spiritus Paraclitus* (Benedictus XV, 1920). G. C. Berkouwer, *De Heilige Schrift*, vol. 1, *Dogmatische Studiën* (Kampen: Kok, 1966), pp. 33–36.

2. Ibid., pp. 32–37.

3. Ibid., p. 190.

4. *"Zo kan ook blijken, dat het in de Schrift niet gaat om een door ons geconstrueerd zekerheidspunt, dat door ons wordt aangegrepen, omdat we in de crisis der zekerheden toch een vaswt, onaantastbaar oriënteringspunt nodig hebben, Zulk een verklaring heft men meermalen gegeven, b.v. toen men in de belijdenis van het Schriftgezag een protestantse parallel meende te zien van het vaste punt in het rooms-katholieke denken nl. De onfeilbaarheid van de paus. Van de protestantse visie op het Schriftgezag gaf men dan een psychologische verklaring—vanuit de behoefte aan een tastbare onwrikbare zekierheidsgrond—en sprak van een papieren paus, een door Lessing gebruikte uitdrukking."*

G. C. Berkouwer, *"Het Schriftgezag,"* in G. C. Berkouwer and A. S. van der Woude, eds., *De Bijbel in het Geding: Een bundel beschouwingen over Schriftkritiek en Schriftgezag* (Nijkerk: Callenbach, 1968), p. 14. English translation by B. Elshout.

5. H. Berkhof, *"De Methode van Berkouwer's Theologie,"* in R. Schippers et al., eds., *Ex Auditu Verbi* (Kampen: Kok, 1965), pp. 44–48.

6. Cornelius Van Til, *In Defense of the Faith,* vol. 1, *The Doctrine of Scripture* (Ripon: Den Dulk Christian Foundation, 1967), p. 148.

7. Ibid., p. 155.

8. *"Ik geloof dat het Schrift minder bang is voor toeschouwers-elementen dan Berkouwer."* Berkhof, *"De Methode van Berkouwer's Theologie,"* p. 55.

9. Cornelius Van Til, *The Defense of the Faith* (Philadelphia: Presbyterian and Reformed, 1955), p. 109.

10. Ibid., p. 179.

11. Ibid., p. 285.

12. W. Ward Fearnside and William B. Hoether, *Fallacy: The Counterfeit of Argument* (Englewood Cliffs: Prentice-Hall, 1959), p. 166.

13. Klaas Runia cites Karl Barth's use of circularity in a favorable way: "The doctrine of Holy Scripture in the Evangelical Church is that this logical circle is the circle of self-asserting, self-attesting truth, into which it is equally impossible to enter as it is to emerge from it: The circle of our freedom, which as such is also the circle of our captivity." Klaas Runia, *Karl Barth's Doctrine of Holy Scripture* (Grand Rapids: Eerdmans, 1962), p. 7.

14. Van Til, *The Defense of the Faith,* p. 101.

15. "It is wholly irrational to hold to any other position than that of Christianity." Ibid., p. 298.

16. See further C. K. Barrett, *Luke the Historian in Recent Study* (London: Epworth, 1961); James Martin, *The Reliability of the Gospels* (London: Hodder and Stoughton, 1959); and F. F. Bruce, *The New Testament Documents: Are They Reliable?* (Chicago: Inter-Varsity, 1943).

17. W. F. Albright and C. S. Mann, *Matthew,* The Anchor Bible (New York: Doubleday, 1971), pp. v–vi.

18. See Helmut Gollwitzer, *The Existence of God as Confessed by Faith*, trans. James W. Leitch (Philadelphia: Westminster, 1965), pp. 146–54.

19. John Calvin, *Institutes of the Christian Religion*, 2 vols., trans. Henry Beveridge (1845; reprint, Grand Rapids: Eerdmans, 1964), 1:72 (1.7.5).

20. Ibid., 1:71 (1.7.4).

21. See G. C. Berkouwer, *De Persoon van Christus, Dogmatische Studiën* (Kampen: Kok, 1952), pp. 178–84.

22. Heinrich Denzinger, ed., *Enchiridion Symbolorum* (Rome: Herder, 1965), para. 2183–85.

23. C. H. Dodd, *The Authority of the Bible* (New York: Harper, 1960), pp. 222–23.

24. Emil Brunner, *The Mediator*, trans. Olive Wyon (Philadelphia: Westminster, 1948), p. 368.

25. Emil Brunner, *Religionsphilosophie* (München, 1927), pp. 77–78; cited by Paul King Jewett in John F. Walvoord, ed., *Inspiration and Interpretation* (Grand Rapids: Eerdmans, 1957), p. 211.

26. See J. I. Packer, *"Fundamentalism" and the Word of God* (Grand Rapids: Eerdmans, 1958), pp. 54–62.

27. James Orr, *Revelation and Inspiration* (1910; reprint, Grand Rapids: Baker, 1969), p. 151.

28. Joachim Jeremias, *New Testament Theology: The Proclamation of Jesus*, trans. John Bowden (New York: Scribners, 1971), p. 206.

29. Ibid., p. 207.

30. Ibid., p. 206.

31. Packer, *"Fundamentalism,"* p. 55.

32. Herman Bavinck writes: *"Deze canon des Ouden Testaments bezat voor Jezus en de apostelen, evanals voor hunne tijdgenooten, goddelijke autoriteit."* Herman Bavinck, *Gereformeerde Dogmatiek*, vol. 1 (Kampen: Bos, 1906), p. 412.

33. *The Constitution of the United Presbyterian Church in the United States of America*, part 1, *Book of Confessions* (Philadelphia: General Assembly Office, 1966), para. 9.26–31.

34. Karl Barth, *Kirchliche Dogmatik*, 1.2.507. Cited in Runia, *Karl Barth's Doctrine of Holy Scripture*, p. 59.

35. Ibid., p. 60.
36. Ibid.
37. Martin Kähler, *The So-Called Historical Jesus and the Historic Biblical Christ*, trans. Carl E. Braaten (Philadelphia: Fortress, 1964), p. 75.
38. James H. Olthuis et al., *Will All the King's Men . . .* (Toronto: Wedge, 1972), p. 183.
39. Edward J. Young, *Thy Word Is Truth: Some Thoughts on the Biblical Doctrine of Inspiration* (Grand Rapids: Eerdmans, 1957), p. 113.
40. Ibid.
41. Ibid.
42. Hans Küng, *Infallible? An Inquiry*, trans. Edward Quinn (New York: Doubleday, 1971), p. 140.
43. Rudolf Bultmann, *"Alētheia,"* in Gerhard Kittel, ed., *Theological Dictionary of the New Testament*, trans. G. W. Bromiley, vol. 1 (Grand Rapids: Eerdmans, 1964).
44. Cyril C. Richardson, ed., *Early Christian Fathers*, trans. Cyril C. Richardson, Library of Christian Classics, vol. 1 (Philadelphia: Westminster, 1953), pp. 370–76.

Chapter 4: The Internal Testimony of the Holy Spirit

1. Benjamin B. Warfield, *The Inspiration and Authority of the Bible*, ed. Samuel G. Craig (Philadelphia: Presbyterian and Reformed, 1948), p. 133.
2. G. C. Berkouwer, *De Heilige Schrift*, vol. 1, *Dogmatische Studiën* (Kampen: Kok, 1966), p. 74.
3. For a survey of modern theological controversy surrounding the *testimonium*, see Bernard Ramm, *The Witness of the Spirit* (Grand Rapids: Eerdmans, 1959).
4. John Calvin, *Institutes of the Christian Religion*, 2 vols., trans. Henry Beveridge (1845; reprint, Grand Rapids: Eerdmans, 1964), 1:68–69 (1.7.1).
5. Ibid., 1:69 (1.7.2).
6. Ibid.
7. Berkouwer, *De Heilige Schrift*, p. 89.
8. See Second Helvetic Confession, chap. 1; Belgic Confession, art. 5; and Westminster Confession, 1.4.5.

9. Calvin, *Institutes*, 1:70 (1.7.3).

10. Ibid., 1:70–71 (1.7.3).

11. Ibid., 1:71 (1.7.4).

12. Ibid.

13. Berkouwer, *De Heilige Schrift*, p. 42.

14. Calvin, *Institutes*, 1:72 (1.7.5).

15. Jim L. McKechnie, ed., *Webster's New Twentieth Century Dictionary*, unabridged ed. (New York: Collins-World, 1975).

16. Ibid.

17. For Adolf Harnack's treatment of the development of the *fides implicitim* in Roman Catholic thought, see his *History of Dogma*, ed. A. B. Bruce, trans. Neil Buchanan et al., 7 vols. (1896–1899; reprint, New York: Dover, 1961), vols. 4–5.

18. Calvin, *Institutes*, 1:71–72 (1.7.4).

19. Ibid., 1:82–83 (1.8.13).

20. Ibid., 1:83 (1.8.13).

21. Benjamin B. Warfield, *Calvin and Augustine*, ed. Samuel G. Craig (Philadelphia: Presbyterian and Reformed, 1956), p. 74.

22. Ibid., p. 87.

23. Ibid., p. 86.

24. Ibid., p. 77.

25. Ibid.

26. Ibid., p. 80.

27. Martin Kähler, *The So-Called Historical Jesus and the Historic Biblical Christ*, trans. Carl E. Braaten (Philadelphia: Fortress, 1964).

28. Emil Brunner, *Revelation and Reason*, trans. Olive Wyon (Philadelphia: Westminster, 1946), pp. 168ff.

29. See Emil Brunner's more comprehensive treatment of this in *The Divine Human Encounter*, trans. Amandus W. Loos (Philadelphia: Westminster, 1943).

30. Compare this concept of "contemporary" with Sören Kierkegaard's concept of the "moment" and Rudolf Bultmann's theology of timelessness with the emphasis on *hic et nunc* encounter.

31. Brunner, *Revelation and Reason*, pp. 170–71.

32. Thomas F. Torrance, "The Epistemological Relevance of the Holy Spirit," in R. Schippers et al., eds., *Ex Auditu Verbi* (Kampen: Kok, 1965), p. 273.

33. Ibid., p. 282.

34. Ibid., p. 283.

35. For an excellent, comprehensive survey of the biblical texts relevant to the discussion, see Ramm, *The Witness of the Spirit*, pp. 42–61.

36. For an exposition of this section, see Philip Edgcumbe Hughes, *Paul's Second Epistle to the Corinthians: The English Text with Introduction, Exposition and Notes* (Grand Rapids: Eerdmans, 1962).

Chapter 7: The Word of God and Inspiration

1. John Calvin, *Institutes of the Christian Religion*, 1.7.1, and *Sermon on Gospel Harmony*, 46:164 and *passim*.

INDEX OF NAMES

205

108, 110, 114, 115, 137, 138, 168, 196 n6, 199 n8, 201 n19, 202 n4, 203 n9 et al., 204 n1
Clement, 47, 48
Clement VI, (Pope), 16
Cochrane, Arthur C., 196 n7
Craig, Samuel G., 195 n1, 202 n1

Daniel, 81, 141
David, 160
Dennison, James T., Jr., 199 n7
Denzinger, Heinrich, 197 n12, 201 n22
Dodd, C. H., 78, 80, 201 n23
Dooyeweerd, Herman, 71
Douglas, J. D., 197 n19

Eck, Johannes von, 16, 24
Edwards, Jonathan, 168
Elijah, 103
Elshout, B., 200 n4
Enoch, 103

Fearnside, W. Ward, 200 n12
Frame, John, 80
Fuller, Reginald H., 199 n9

Galileo, 153
George, (Duke), 17
Gerstner, John, 41–42
Giger, George Musgrave, 199 n7
Gollwitzer, Helmut, 201 n18
Gregory I, (Pope), 78
Grimm, Harold J., 195 n2

Harnack, Adolf, 203 n17
Harrison, Everett F., 48, 199 n4

Harrison, R. K., 50, 199 n6
Harvey, Van, 198 n25
Hegel, Georg W. F., 69
Heidegger, Martin, 55, 114
Heppe, Heinrich, 15, 21, 195 n1
Hodge, A. A., 25, 27, 36
Hoether, William B., 200 n12
Hollaz, David, 108
Hughes, Philip Edgcumbe, 204 n36
Huss, John, 17

Ignatius, 47
Irenaeus, 46, 89
Isaiah, 81

James, 84, 141
Jeremiah, 81
Jeremias, Joachim, 81, 201 n28
Jesus, 20, 22, 39, 43, 44, 45–46, 50, 51, 53, 72–73, 75, 77–82, 84–85, 87, 88, 89, 103, 110, 115, 128, 130, 145–46, 160, 163–66, 175, 177, 184, 186, 187, 188–90, 193, 197 n16, 198 n25, 201 n32
Jewett, Paul King, 198 n26, 201 n25
John XXIII, (Pope), 24, 197 n13
Jonah, 160
Josephus, 51
Justin Martyr, 47

Kähler, Martin, 86, 110, 202 n37, 203 n27
Kierkegaard, Sören, 112, 203 n30
Kittel, Gerhard, 202 n43

Küng, Hans, 88–89, 196 n5, 202 n42

Kuyper, Abraham, 62, 68, 72

Leitch, James W., 201 n18
Leo XIII, (Pope), 199 n1
Lessing, Gotthold Ephraim, 65
Lindsell, Harold, 28, 30, 197 n21
Loos, Amandus W., 203 n29
Lovelace, Richard, 28, 197 n19
Luke, 47, 141
Luther, Martin, 16–18, 20, 24, 27, 40–41, 42, 52, 61, 86, 115, 123–24, 168, 171, 196 n4, 196 n6

Machen, J. Gresham, 8
McKechnie, Jim L., 202 n15
Malachi, 51
Mann, C. S., 74, 200 n17
Marcion, 47, 53
Mark, 81
Marsden, George, 195 n4
Martin, James, 200 n16
Matthew, 141
Melanchthon, Phillip, 15
Montgomery, John Warwick, 9, 77, 195 n6, 196 n6, 197 n17
Moses, 79, 84, 137, 160, 165, 187
Murray, Iain H., 195 n5
Murray, John, 80

Nacchianti, (Bishop), 23
Nicole, Roger, 80

Olthuis, James H., 202 n38
Origen, 49

Orr, James, 80, 201 n27

Packer, J. I., 27–28, 80, 81, 196 n6, 197 n17, 201 n26, 201 n31
Papias, 47
Paul, 36, 45, 46, 47, 48, 84, 94, 108, 116–17, 163
Peter, 46, 47, 48, 115
Pinnock, Clark, 80
Plato, 103
Polycarp, 47

Quenstedt, Johannes Andreas, 106
Quinn, Edward, 196 n5, 202 n42

Ramm, Bernard, 25–27, 30–32, 197 n14, 197 n22, 202 n3, 204 n35
Richardson, Cyril C., 202 n44
Roberts, Oral, 59
Robertson, Pat, 59
Rogers, Jack, 197 n14
Runia, Klaas, 200 n13, 201 n34
Rupp, Gordon, 16, 196 n3

Sadolet(o), Jacopo, 92
Schaeffer, Francis, 28–30, 197 n19, 197 n20
Schippers, R., 200 n5, 203 n32
Schleiermacher, Friedrich, 74
Schroeder, H. J., 196 n9
Schultz, Robert C., 196 n4
Schweitzer, Albert, 53
Socrates, 102–3
Sproul, R. C., 8–10, 195 n7
Stonehouse, Ned B., 195 n2

INDEX OF SCRIPTURE

209

R. C. Sproul (Drs., Free University of Amsterdam) is the founder and chairman of Ligonier Ministries, serves as senior minister of preaching and teaching at St. Andrews Chapel, Sanford, Florida, and is the teacher on Ligonier's daily radio program, *Renewing Your Mind.* He has written more than sixty books, including *The Holiness of God, Faith Alone, Chosen by God, What is Reformed Theology?, The Glory of Christ, The Mystery of the Holy Spirit,* and *Getting the Gospel Right.* He is also editor of *The Reformation Study Bible,* which has been published with the New King James Version and with the English Standard Version.